ALL THE GEAR, NO IDEA

A woman's solo motorbike journey around the
Indian subcontinent

by Michèle Harrison

To John, Allie and Tom

Author's note

Every year hundreds of foreigners tour India on Enfield Bullets – classic British-designed motorbikes still manufactured in India. Most, however, are experienced riders.

I'd only ridden mopeds around London when I decided in 1997 to spend nearly a year travelling around the Indian subcontinent on an Enfield 500cc. My 17,000-mile (27,000-km) journey, which took place between October 1997 and September 1998, took me through the mayhem of Delhi traffic, the mountains of Kashmir, the deserts of Rajasthan, the beaches of Goa, the southern tip of India, the remote tracks of Nepal and the eerie Himalayan barrenness of Ladakh.

This book came out of a diary I kept on my travels. In order to protect their anonymity, I've changed the names and identifying features of some – but not all – of the characters I met that appear within these pages.

This journey started simply as a way of spicing up a boring life and fulfilling my wanderlust; of course, it ended up being much more than that.

I hope the reader will experience, as I did, the thrills of riding a gorgeous machine – one that hasn't changed much since the 1950s – through a beautiful and mysterious country.

Acknowledgement (updated edition, 2015)

Although all remaining inaccuracies and mistakes are very much my responsibility, I would like to thank my copy editor, Georgia Laval (Laval Editing), for her help in this much improved edition.

Contents

Map of journey

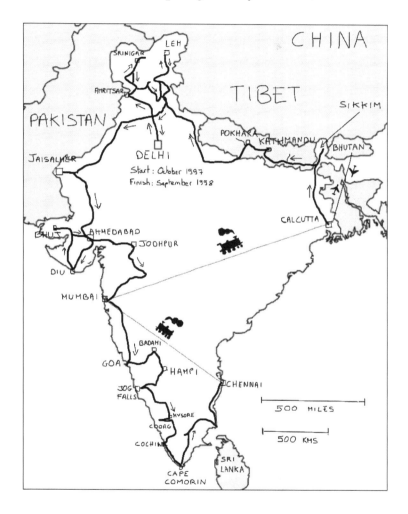

Chapter 1
In your face

'So Daniel, why are we meeting in this pub?' I asked, as I pushed the overflowing ashtray away from me.

'We're meeting here because I don't like your West End wine bars filled with boring old suits,' Daniel answered. 'And besides, they have a really big TV screen here.'

I sighed. So *that* was the real reason – football. Spain versus England.

The referee whistled for the start of the match, but I refused to let Daniel watch in peace. I was determined to continue the subject we'd started on the underground. 'So, what do you think I should do about my job?'

Daniel – my ex-boyfriend and now a good friend – eventually looked away from the screen and towards me.

'Look Michèle, I've known you for three years and you've always talked about quitting your job. If you're bored with it, pack it in!'

'I know. You're right. But I don't know what else to do.'

'So what?' He shrugged. 'If I were you, I'd just quit.'

He turned back to the screen just in time to see England lose the ball.

'You should just piss off for a while... I don't know... travel.'

'But that's just temporary. What about the rest of my life?' I whined.

'Christ, I don't know! But things happen when you travel: things change, *you* change. You meet new people, you get new ideas. And before you know it your whole life has changed.'

He looked down at his empty pint. 'Isn't it your turn to buy?'

When I returned with his pint of house best and my gin and tonic, Daniel was totally engrossed in the football match again. My interest in football was limited to comparing the looks of the players, and although the Spanish team was very good-looking, my mind wandered.

I felt unsettled. Maybe Daniel was right. I'd been in the investment management business in London for 10 years, always thinking that one day I'd leave to do something else but always too afraid to do it.

'If you were me, where would you go?' I asked.

Immersed, he hadn't heard me.

'Daniel – where would you go?'

'I don't know... anywhere... somewhere different. Maybe Latin America or Africa. Or what about India? Lots of people speak English there and it's supposed to be really "in your face".'

'What do you mean, "in your face"?' I asked.

'You know – intense. Lots of cultural shock. That kind of stuff.'

The noise in the pub rose to a crescendo but soon abated to a groan when the England team failed to score from a promising corner. Daniel rolled his eyes.

'Want another drink?' I asked.

He'd barely started his second pint but I was already crunching on my ice cubes.

He laughed. 'Michèle, you're a piss-head.'

'Yep, and I'm going to get another.'

Leaving Daniel to his football, I walked over to the bar and ordered my drink. No point in going back to him, I thought – he's only interested in the match and I'm too tense to sit down, let alone watch football.

Instead I stood in front of the bar, which was now deserted as everyone was watching the match on the other side of the room.

He's right, I thought. I should just resign. Simple as that.

Just to see what it sounded like, I whispered, 'I'm resigning.'

It didn't sound too bad.

I repeated it, a bit louder this time: 'I'm resigning on Monday.'

It still sounded quite good.

Then louder still: 'I'm going to go to my boss on Monday and I'm going to hand in my resignation!'

'You do that, luv!' the barman laughed.

I rushed back to our table.

'That's it, I've decided. I'm really going to resign this time,' I announced.

'That's good,' Daniel replied, still staring at the screen.

His pinched look told me the match was not going well for England.

~~~~~~~~~~~~

Now, apart from a job, I also had a boyfriend. Matthew was a lawyer and a lovely man, but not one that'd want to go off to India. The two of us were going to York that weekend to visit the grave of his father, who had died exactly one year previously. Not the best time to announce I was leaving.

We took the train up North and had a lonely weekend; Matthew because he was caught up in memories of his father and all the things he wished he'd said to him before he died, and me because I was preoccupied with my imminent announcement and how much it could hurt him.

Once we'd boarded the train back to London I gathered my courage and broached the subject.

'Matthew?'

'Yes?'

'I've got something to tell you.' Matthew put down his copy of *The Law Review* and turned his attention to me.

'I've decided I'm going to resign from my job tomorrow. I don't know exactly what I'll do after I've finished but I've three months' notice to work it out. I'll probably go travelling for a while, maybe in India.'

I added, 'Actually, I was reading the *Lonely Planet* guide to India and it seems lots of people buy Enfield motorbikes to tour the country. The bikes are called Bullets.'

I knew Matthew used to ride motorbikes in his early 20s so I thought this might impress him.

'Obviously I've never ridden a motorbike, but they can't be that different from mopeds, eh?' I laughed nervously.

Never the talkative type, Matthew closed his eyes and leaned back into his seat.

Never the quiet type, I continued. 'Look, I don't know how we'll feel about each other when I come back. I know it's a risk but it's something I really want to do. I just feel like my life has been stagnating and I want to try something new.'

Oh no, that didn't sound good.

'I don't mean I haven't been happy in our relationship, or that I want to find someone else. It's just... well, you know... I feel... Look, I'm sorry about this. Why aren't you saying anything?'

Still leaning back in his chair, Matthew turned his head towards me and said, 'I hope this isn't just a complicated way of getting rid of me.'

~~~~~~~~~~~

Monday morning, in the bank where I worked. Resignation Day.

I was scared without really knowing why. It seemed much more difficult than I'd imagined, when all I had to do was walk into my boss's office and say the words.

Instead I kept finding papers to file, phone calls to make.

Finally I took a deep breath and entered his office.

David looked up: 'Is it time for our meeting already?' he asked.

Shit. I'd waited so long it was now 10.30am – the time of our Monday meeting.

'Right then,' he started. 'What do we have to cover?'

Another deep breath.

'Look, David. I've got something to tell you.'

I closed the door to his office and sat in the leather chair opposite his desk.

'I've… er… I've decided to resign.'

My boss looked up but said nothing. (Another quiet type.)

I fumbled through my black folder and pulled out an envelope. 'Here's my letter of resignation.'

I placed it on his desk and we both looked at its smooth surface.

Finally David reached out to pick the envelope up. 'I see,' he said.

I see? Is that all? What about the bit where he begs me to reconsider? What about the bit where he asks if there's anything he can do to make me change my mind? I wanted to be able to say to him, gently but firmly, 'It's really nice of you to ask, and I'm flattered, but my mind's made up and nothing you can say will change it.'

But no. All I got was 'I see.'

As I opened the door to leave his office, David asked me the one question I'd been dreading. 'Any particular reason you're leaving?'

What could I tell him? That I was bored out of my mind and at the same time far too stressed? That I didn't like wearing suits (even nice ones)? That I felt my life was passing me by while I worried about how to make rich people richer? That I was afraid this was what life was all about – and would ever be about – for me?

I shrugged and answered, 'No, just personal stuff.'

There was someone else at work I had to tell: my assistant Kathryn – a very efficient, lively and attractive brunette. We'd worked very well together for the past three years and I felt a bit like I was deserting her.

I shouldn't have worried.

When I told her over lunch at a nearby Japanese restaurant, she exclaimed, 'Michèle, that's so exciting! How brilliant for you! And to tell you the truth, I've also been thinking of trying something completely different. So this will give me another reason to do something about changing *my* career!'

She took a sip of wine and continued, 'Do you have any idea what you'll do?'

'First I'll go to India and buy myself a motorcycle – a Royal Enfield Bullet – and then I'll go off touring.' I replied. 'And after that, who knows?' I gave a shrug, and then added, 'But I hope never to work in finance again.'

Kathryn laughed and the men at the next table turned to look. 'To be honest, Michèle, I'm not really surprised. I never had you down as the fund manager type!'

At my leaving do the office presented me with a t-shirt emblazoned with the words, 'BABE ON A BULLET.'

Chapter 2
The test

'Where the hell *are* they?' I asked myself.

It was nine o'clock in the morning and the three-day intensive motorcycle course was supposed to start at eight thirty. But I was the only mug there, sitting under the drizzle on the steps to the padlocked door of a motorcycle school in Crystal Palace Park, getting increasingly annoyed.

I decided to call the school's head office in Brighton to see what was going on, and found a payphone nearby. No answer. Typical – the office probably didn't open until nine thirty.

I began to suspect the whole set-up was a con job: they'd put an ad in *Motorcycle News* for a three-day course, raked in all the deposits and disappeared. Looking back, they'd been very prompt in cashing my deposit...

A panic rose in me: my flight to Delhi was in four weeks and I needed to learn how to ride a motorbike and get a licence by then. I'd have to book with another school and hope to pass on the first attempt.

I decided to go home and get on the phone rather than waste any more time standing around in the rain. I set off walking back towards the train station, but soon spotted a park attendant.

'Excuse me,' I asked him, 'can you tell me if there's motorcycle school operating out of this building?'

'Yes, that's a council school, but they've been closed since the summer. You'll be wanting the private one.'

He pointed to the left. 'It's behind those trees.'

I ran over to find a single-storey prefab building surrounded by a fence with a big locked gate.

'Hello – anybody there?' I shouted.

I could see a motorbike outside a shed. A large man

who looked to be in his 30s came out of the building dressed in black bike leathers.

'Hi! Are you Barry, the instructor?'

'Yes?' He approached the fence.

'I'm booked on your course; I was waiting at the other motorcycle school and only just found you.'

'Oh! I was just closing up: I figured you weren't coming and put the bike back in the shed,' Barry said as he unlocked the gate. 'You're late, but since you're the only one signed up for the course we should be able to catch up on lost time. If you're good at following instructions, that is…'

He fetched the bike out of the shed. A Honda CB600. Wow! It certainly looked a lot more impressive than my Vespa.

I was eager to try it out, but Barry led me to the prefab building and proceeded to deliver two hours of motorcycle theory: how to choose a helmet, what the various bits of the bike were and how they worked, how to position the bike on the road, and when to do a life-saver (i.e. when to check over my shoulder). Answer: all the time.

We then went out to the parking lot where I practiced pushing the very heavy bike around and familiarised myself with the controls.

Finally I climbed onto the saddle, checked I was in neutral and pressed the start button. The engine came to life.

'Okay,' Barry said. 'Now, engage your clutch with your left hand, press your left foot down to change into first gear, and slowly release the clutch lever as you give it a bit of throttle with your right hand.' With a frown he added, 'Did you get that, darling?'

Hmmm, I thought, *I'll show him.* I decided to impress him with a bit of clutch control. I slowly released the clutch, turned the throttle… and almost fell off the bike as the engine gave out a roar and the front wheel lifted off the ground. I swear, it wasn't intentional, but I'd just done my first wheelie.

Barry, however, was not impressed.

'Look, none of this shit here. Acrobatics are for show-offs and teenagers – neither of which should be riding motorbikes.'

'I didn't mean to – really,' I blabbered. 'I thought I'd only given it a twinge on the throttle.'

Clearly unconvinced, Barry made me spend the rest of the day practising in the rain in the parking lot. I rode the bike at walking pace, did figures of eight, turned right, turned left and did emergency stops.

The following day, complete with one-way radios in our helmets, we hit the road. Barry followed me on his bike and gave me directions: 'Turn left'; 'Turn right'; 'Go straight over the roundabout'; 'Make sure you're in the correct lane as you approach the roundabout'; 'Check your speed'; 'Don't forget to switch off your indicator after you've completed your turn'; 'Watch out for the bicycle.'

Things were going reasonably well – or so I thought – when he brought me to a quiet residential street and asked me to do a U-turn without putting my foot down. The more I tried, the more difficult I found it. Eventually I wobbled, lost my balance and fell over.

Barry quickly dismounted from his bike and ran over to help me lift mine back up.

'It helps if you put your weight slightly more over to the outside of your bike. And you mustn't look at the curb.' He continued, 'Look in the direction that you want to go in. If you look at the curb you'll end up pointing at it instead of at the road. Okay, let's try again.'

After what he'd said about looking at the curb, this time, of course, I couldn't do anything *but* look straight at it, and ended up bumping into it and almost falling down again in the process.

'Never mind,' he said to me over the radio. 'I think we'd better call it a day.'

Oh, no! I thought. My test was the following afternoon and the U-turn was compulsory.

~~~~~~~~~~~~~

The next morning the Honda was out for repairs – our fall had caused damage to more than just my confidence – and Barry put me on a Kawasaki GT550. We stayed in the parking lot for an hour as I got used to it, and then rode down to Biggin Hill via some winding country lanes.

Suddenly I heard Barry on the radio. '*Shit*, I made a mistake: we should've taken the previous right. Turn back and take the first left.'

I did just that.

'Hehe! Not a bad U-turn!' he laughed into my earphone.

We rode back up towards London and approached the test centre in Greenwich. During a final check to ensure I understood the various controls on the bike, we discovered that the horn didn't work. Barry tried twiddling with the various wires but couldn't get it repaired; we just had to hope a little old blind lady didn't walk out in front of the bike during the test…

Despite a rather wobbly U-turn, I passed the test; and although a little old lady did cross in front of me, she did so on a zebra crossing and I'd stopped well in advance. Little did I know then that in India the horn would turn out to be my most vital safety tool.

~~~~~~~~~~~~~

The next four weeks were spent finishing up at work, saying goodbye to my friends and meticulously planning what I'd take with me on my journey. The aim was to carry only hand luggage on the plane: no make-up, no jewellery, only two pair of trousers, one t-shirt and one sweatshirt. I could buy whatever I needed when I got to India. And anyway, who needed a towel when you could dry yourself with a sarong that could also serve as a skirt, a scarf and a bed sheet?

Many happy hours were spent choosing the best backpack, the thinnest motorcycle gloves and the thermal leggings with the best weight-to-warmth ratio.

I was ready for my journey.

Chapter 3
Buying the bike in Delhi

I remember how, that first night in Delhi, I lay awake in my tiny hotel room, my damp body pressed into the damp sheets, wondering what lay ahead of me and thinking it would just about be time in London for my colleagues to be leaving the office. Or rather my *ex*-colleagues.

I remember listening to my churning stomach while the flickering neon light reflected off the wet walls of the windowless room. Instead of windows, my hotel room had brick-sized holes over the door. If they were meant to provide some ventilation in the room, they weren't succeeding. Not a very good choice of hotel on my part; I decided I'd have to find something better soon.

Still, the cab ride from the airport had been quite enjoyable, and the roads were in reasonable condition. But then so they should be: it was the main route between the airport and the capital, after all.

The taxi was an old white Morris Oxford-like car – an Ambassador – and the driver, who barely looked of a legal age to drive, didn't speak much English and had no idea how to get to my hotel. Neither did he carry a plan of the city, so I ended up directing him, at ten o'clock at night, using the map in my guidebook.

Sitting on the sticky plastic of the back seat of the car, I looked out the window, searching for my first sight of an Enfield; but apart from scooters, the biggest two-wheeler I spotted was a Kawasaki 100. Most riders wore helmets – although some only had yellow plastic construction site hats – and many scooters carried two passengers, almost always helmet-less.

Before I'd left England, an Indian friend had explained to me that although driving in India would seem chaotic at the beginning, there were rules to it. The only problem was that these rules weren't to be found in any highway code manual – so my safety would depend on figuring them out as soon as possible.

With that in mind, I looked out of the taxi and quickly identified the following traffic rules:

- You can go through red lights as long as you're confident that the lights on the other side have not yet changed to green.
- If a vehicle in front of you is moving too slowly, you can go onto the hard shoulder and overtake it on the inside.
- When driving at night, you should turn off your headlights wherever there are street lamps in order to save your batteries (or is it your lightbulbs?).
- You should press on your horn at least four times a minute in moving traffic, and significantly more in stationary traffic.

We reached my hotel at around eleven o'clock at night and I thought, rather disappointedly, that we were in the suburbs – it was so quiet, and there didn't seem to be any shop fronts. But the next morning the street came to life: shutters opened up, and shops spilled over onto the pavement. A large parking lot for motorcycles had materialized right outside the hotel entrance; the road was packed with vehicles and traffic was at a standstill. Hundreds of pedestrians walked on the street, weaving between the cars, the buses, the trucks, the auto-rickshaws, the scooters, the bicycles and the odd cow.

I could taste the dust and the diesel fumes that hung above us in a dense haze, dimming the sun's rays.

I checked out of my hotel and switched to the nearby YMCA, where I had to sign a commitment not to have men or alcoholic drinks in my room. Next, I set out looking for a hairdresser. I'd decided that because of the heat and humidity I'd need short hair for wearing a helmet. A new beginning, after all, demands a new look.

After an hour of wandering around the streets asking (or rather gesturing) for directions, I was led into a tailor's shop. It seemed my 'haircut' gesture had been mistaken for 'made-to-measure'. I turned around to leave, but the tailor stopped me.

'Can I help you, madam?' he asked.

'Actually, no. I'm sorry, I was looking for a hairdresser.'

'Yes, yes. Come in, madam.'

I followed him into the back of the shop to a tiny cubicle where a young barber was beating up one of his clients – or so it seemed.

Noticing my puzzled expression, the tailor/barber explained: 'The slaps on the scalp and face are to stimulate circulation.'

I came out some time later with very rosy cheeks and a man's haircut.

Just around the corner I spotted a hand-written sign advertising an office with e-mail access. The building was in a back street of beaten earth, with open sewers on both sides and cows meandering among the pedestrians and parked cars. Inside, a young woman dressed in a royal blue sari showed me how to log onto the computer. I looked down at her hands on the keyboard and noticed she had a sixth lifeless finger dangling from the side of her palm. I tried to act nonchalant but my eyes kept returning to the limp digit with its carefully manicured and varnished crimson nail.

The computer terminals rested on narrow desks with the keyboards precariously balanced on open drawers. On the floor, two brown mice played hide-and-seek behind the hard disk drives. Still, there was air-conditioning and the connection to the internet only broke down twice.

And so on my first day I managed to send e-mails home: 'Hot and humid in Delhi. Traffic is mad. Thousands of people in the streets. All the men have moustaches and all the women wear beautiful colours.'

~~~~~~~~~~

In the afternoon I decided to go to the Enfield dealer. Even though part of me wanted to wait a bit longer and get used to my new surroundings, I feared that the longer I waited to buy the motorbike, the more likely I was to give up on the whole idea.

I called the dealer from the YMCA.

'Mr Singh? Hello, it's Michèle Harrison here. I called you from England the day before yesterday, about an Enfield 500. I'm now here in Delhi and was wondering if it would be convenient for me to come over.'

A pause.

'Mr Singh?'

A deep voice replied, 'Yes... this afternoon is... fine. You know how to get here?'

I pulled out my map of Delhi. 'I just know it's in Karol Bagh. If I show your address to an auto-rickshaw driver, will he know it?'

'Yes, just ask for Jhandi Wallah Extension.'

After I'd hung up I went over to the YMCA's reception counter.

'Can you tell me where I can find a rickshaw?' I asked the receptionist – a young woman dressed in a bright pink sari and wearing a crucifix around her neck.

She answered, 'There are a number of rickshaw drivers waiting outside the hotel, but they are not honest people. They will not use their meter and will overcharge you. You should try to hail a rickshaw in the street instead.'

'How much will it cost me if I use one of the rickshaws outside the YMCA?' I asked.

'They will probably ask you for 50 rupees, but the correct price should be 30 rupees.'

I decided to go for the dishonest option: it was only $1.50, after all.

Outside the YMCA I found a row of auto-rickshaws. Half a dozen drivers were sitting on a low wall, chatting together and chewing red betel nuts. They stood up as soon as I appeared. The tallest man, good-looking in a rather decadent way, with fleshy features and full lips glistening with the red betel juices, approached me.

'Where would you like to go, young madam?' he asked with a slight leer, while placing his right hand protectively over his balls as though he feared they might roll onto the road.

'Karol Bagh. Do you know it?'

'Ah! Karol Bagh is specialising in two-wheelers.' His hand was now gently stroking the seam at his crotch. 'You will be looking for a scooter, madam?'

'No, not a scooter – an Enfield motorcycle.' I replied, trying not to show him I'd noticed he even *had* balls. I then added, indicating to the first vehicle in the line, 'Is this your auto-rickshaw?'

'No,' he pointed the other way with his chin. 'This one here is my rickshaw.'

'Well, sorry, I'll be taking the first rickshaw in the queue. Where's the driver of this one?'

'He's not here, madam.'

I approached the vehicle and found the driver asleep in the back seat with a newspaper over his face to keep the flies away.

'Excuse me, can you take me to Karol Bagh?'

Startled, he jumped up and fixed his blood-shot gaze on me.

'Karol Bagh?' I repeated.

'No problem,' he replied as he leapt over into the driver's seat.

'How much?' I asked.

He smiled, showing me his betel-stained gums. 'No problem.'

'The hotel told me 50 rupees. Is that okay?'

'No problem.'

As soon as I'd sat down he started his engine and sharply pulled out into the traffic, tossing me against the canvas wall of his rickshaw.

Holding on tightly to the single bar that acted as a door, I shouted a question to him over the noise of the engine and the constant blowing of his horn.

'Do you know Mandi Motors?'

No answer.

'It's in Jhandi Wallah Extension!' I cried out.

He turned his head around but kept the full weight of his foot on the accelerator pedal and his finger firmly pressed on the horn button.

'Jhandi Wallah Extension?'

'Yes.'

'No problem.'

Obviously very few things were a problem to this man: red lights were no problem – he went through them; cows in the middle of the road were no problem – he swerved around them; terrified groups of tourists were no problem – he ploughed through them.

Suddenly he came to a screeching halt and pointed to the other side of a very busy road. (Granted, they're all very busy roads in Delhi, but this was a *very* busy road.) 'Jhandi Wallah Extension,' he announced.

'Can you bring me right up to Mandi Motors? I don't know where it is.'

'No English,' he replied.

'Mandi Motors.' I handed him a piece of paper. 'Look, here's the address.'

'No English,' he repeated.

'*Please* bring me to Mandi Motors,' I pleaded.

I feared I'd never survive crossing the road, let alone find the shop once I got to the other side.

Obviously annoyed, the driver snatched the piece of paper out of my hand and walked over to a man sitting on the pavement offering his services as a zip repairer. They spoke, and then the driver climbed back into the auto-rickshaw and did the tightest U-turn in history, knocking my head against the bar in the process. Twice more he stopped abruptly to ask directions, and he eventually delivered me, slightly shaken, to Mandi Motors, the official Enfield dealer in the Indian capital.

It was a small shop on a corner, with a dozen used

motorbikes parked in front on the road. A teenaged, oil-covered mechanic was crouching outside the shop front, looking mournfully at the skeleton of a motorbike and its disembowelled guts lying on the ground.

I walked into the shop. My attention was immediately drawn to a beautiful, brand new Enfield leaning against the back wall. It leapt out against the shabbiness of the store with its shiny metallic grey/green paintwork, its glistening chrome finish, its elegant teardrop-shaped tank and its old fashioned-looking engine. It was as if it had just come out of a Second World War film set; the only thing missing was a side-car for the radio operator.

'Yes?' a man's voice interrupted my reverie. 'You are wanting?'

'Is Mr Singh here?' I asked.

He pointed to a large man with a big red turban talking to a Western man in the corner.

I approached them.

'Mr Singh?'

He nodded.

'I called you earlier about buying an Enfield 500.'

'Ah, yes. Could you sit down for a moment and wait a little bit? Would you like some tea?'

Before I could answer he shouted 'Chai!' to the mechanic outside who very soon afterwards brought me a cup of sweet, strong and very milky tea. I hate milk in my tea. I thanked him and drank it as fast as I could to get rid of the taste. Unfortunately, the young man interpreted this as a desire for a refill.

As I sat in the shop I could hear the Westerner – a Belgian man, according to the mechanic – arguing with Mr Singh.

'You told me I could 'ave an Enfield 500cc this week. I 'ave bin waitin' three weeks, you know? Now you say non!? Mais, c'est pas possible, ça!'

'I understand you are having a problem but you see this lady ordered this bike from England for delivery today.'

'So why didn't you tell me this before, hein?'

'Well I didn't know if she was really going to come. I am so very sorry. I can get you a 350cc immediately if you want.'

'No, I don't want a stupid 350!' the Belgian shouted as he stormed out of the shop.

Mr Singh turned to me and said, with a gentle smile, 'I am thinking this man is not very happy.' He continued, 'I have your bike here. Will you be wishing to register the vehicle in your name?'

'Well, yes,' I replied, surprised.

He rummaged through a pile of papers on a table and pulled one out.

'In that case you must get a letter from your embassy confirming you are a permanent resident in India registered at this address,' he said as he handed me the address.

'Oh really? Why?' I asked.

'If you break the law, the police must be able to locate you.'

'And what address is this?'

'It does not exist,' he answered smiling. 'Come back tomorrow when you have the letter.'

~~~~~~~~~~

That evening I had dinner in the YMCA's restaurant and the bill came to 107 rupees. I offered 200 rupees to the waiter, but he wanted the exact money. By emptying all my pockets I was able to come up with 106 rupees – just one short (one rupee is worth one third of a US cent).

'Will you take 106 rupees?' I asked.

'No, I will go look for some change,' he replied.

After ten minutes he returned with a disappointed look on his face.

'Can you check again for one more rupee?' he asked. 'We are not having change.'

'I've checked already,' I smiled apologetically. 'I'm

sorry but I don't have one.'

A middle-aged Indian man eating at the table next to mine leaned over and said, 'Please allow me to give you the missing rupee. As you can see there is a big shortage of change in India.'

~~~~~~~~~~

As instructed by the Enfield dealer, the next morning I went to the British embassy and was surprised at how easy it was to get the letter. All I had to do was tell them I wanted to buy a motorcycle and that I lived at the fictitious address. No questions asked.

The woman behind the counter was very friendly and told me about a salon in the diplomatic area of Delhi where I could get beauty treatments. My short hair was depressing me, and the idea of some girly pampering appealed. So later, for just $15 I had a manicure, pedicure and a facial. The facial was amazing: the woman massaged my face, neck and shoulder for probably half an hour. The young girl who did my hands also massaged my arms. I felt *so* relaxed and clean by the time they'd finished.

Unfortunately the cleanliness didn't last. The auto-rickshaw I travelled back to the town centre in got stuck behind a diesel fume-spewing truck. Even my driver was coughing.

Then we slowly passed a gruesome sight: a blanket-covered human body in the inside lane. It wasn't covered very well and I could see a pool of blood just by the edge, and what looked like a piece of a jaw with teeth still attached to it.

~~~~~~~~~~

When I returned to the dealer that afternoon with the letter from the embassy, I also brought 60,000 rupees ($1,600) in cash – the price of a brand new Enfield 500 including insurance, road tax, panniers, leg frames and mirrors.

Although the largest bills in India are for 500 rupees ($15), they are very hard to find. Even 100 rupee bills are often scarce. When I went to the bank to change my foreign currency, the teller only had 50 and 100 rupee bills, and so it was with eight huge stacks of the equivalent one and a half and three dollar bills that I arrived at the dealer.

After handing over the money, I expected to receive the keys to the bike.

'No, madam. It is not finished. We need to get the road tax, the registration papers and the comprehensive insurance. I will send one of my boys to do it for you.'

'So the bike's not mine, yet? But I just paid you all the money!'

'You are worried I am trying to cheat you?'

Well, I thought, my guidebook is full of dire warnings about con jobs, and it specifically warns motorbike buyers not to hand over the money until they get the keys.

'Er… can I go with the boy to get the proper documentation?' I asked.

'Of course, but there are many offices to visit, and they will ask more questions about your residency if you are there,' he warned.

'Okay, never mind,' I answered. Then I added, as much to reassure myself as to warn him, 'I do have a receipt from you after all.'

'Do not worry. Come tomorrow afternoon around four o'clock and everything will be ready.'

He was right. The next day I became the proud owner of a gorgeous, gleaming Royal Enfield 500. I was now officially a real biker.

With much excitement I approached my bike outside the shop and inserted the key in the ignition. The adventure was about to begin. I kicked the start lever to start the engine and… nothing. I checked that the key was fully turned, the petrol lever at the ON position, and the choke out. I kicked again. Again, nothing. And again, and again, and again. Not even a cough out of the engine.

I felt extremely hot in the afternoon sun, and the presence of a group of young men on the pavement watching me intently was not helping. Eventually I gave up and walked back into the shop to ask for help, and Mr Singh offered to start my bike. It fired at his first attempt. He dismounted and invited me to take over.

Then he hesitated and asked, 'Would you like my mechanic to ride it back to your hotel?'

I nodded in shame.

And so I suffered the indignity of riding pillion on my own motorcycle behind a child mechanic too young to have a licence.

Once back at the YMCA's parking lot and away from onlookers, it only took about a dozen attempts and a few floodings of the engine to get it started again. I rode slowly around the car park and thought, 'Hey! That's not so hard!' Even so, on Mr Singh's advice, I decided to stay in Delhi for a few days to practise riding the bike in the early hours of the morning when the traffic would be lighter.

Then I went to a tailor to have an outfit made for me, since I'd only brought two sets of clothes. It was an Indian design – a punjabi – that consisted of a pair of narrow yellow trousers and a navy blue tunic. I chose an Indian style because I'd heard that in the countryside Western women in Western clothes often got a lot of hassle. I found the measurement-taking rather embarrassing, as at 5'10" I'm not exactly small, even by Western standards. Quite a contrast to the Indian saleswoman who, if she'd been in the West, would have had to buy her clothes in the children's department.

The next day, at six o'clock in the morning, I went out to practise my riding in the quiet streets of Delhi. Actually, that's a lie: I just rode my motorcycle around and around Connaught Place – a large roundabout – because I was afraid of getting lost. By seven-thirty the traffic was already too heavy for me and I returned to the YMCA.

My first attempt at riding on Indian roads had not been very impressive. The engine had stalled a lot, and each time I'd pulled over to try and kick-start the bike I'd felt intimidated by an audience of ten or twenty people that'd materialised around me. Another problem was that I constantly confused my foot brake with the gears – they're the 'wrong' way around on an Enfield – which meant that every time I'd wanted to stop I'd ended up changing gear instead (without the clutch) and, of course, stalling.

When I arrived back at the YMCA for breakfast I met another resident: Sonny – a British man of Indian origins who'd worked as a bike courier in London. He was in his late twenties, wore a black baseball cap, a tight black t-shirt, baggy jeans and a pair of brilliant-white Nike sports shoes.

Feeling more confident in his company, I went out for a ride on my Enfield with Sonny sitting behind me. However, we'd barely set off when he ordered me to stop.

He laughed, 'You don't know about the gears on an Enfield, do you?'

'What do you mean?' I responded defensively, 'I know they're under the right foot instead of the left one.'

'Yeah, that's true. But they're also one up and three down, not one down and three up.'

'I don't understand.'

'Here, let me show you.'

I dismounted and Sonny took my place.

'See, the Enfield is different from modern bikes. To get into first gear you need to bring up the foot lever with your toes, but to get into second gear you press down on the pedal. You also press down for third and fourth. That's why your riding is so jerky. You've been changing from neutral into second gear and then accelerating into first!'

I didn't dare ask him what kind of damage this must have caused the engine.

Another useful thing my ex-courier friend showed me was how to get onto the highway that went to the city of Amritsar, my next destination. By this time I was really itching to get out of Delhi and start my journey. Furthermore, the longer I stayed in Delhi, the more scared

I was getting about the whole idea.

The next day, in the hotel's parking lot, I practised putting the bike on its centre stand. This supposedly requires more technique than strength, but at that stage I had no technique and so relied totally on muscle power. First and second attempts were successful, but at the third attempt I was so tired that I dropped the bike. Fortunately a young man who'd just parked his car rushed to help me.

While we were picking the bike up he asked me, 'You want to sell your bike? I give you good price.'

'No, I just bought it,' I laughed.

'How much did you pay for it?' he asked.

'I bought it new,' I said, 'for 60,000 rupees.'

'60,000 rupees! That is very expensive. I think maybe they cheated you because you are a foreigner.'

I later learned not to give the true price of the bike, because people seldom believed it was really new – which just confirmed their view that I was a stupid foreigner with too much money.

There was a little surface damage to the bike, and the leg frame was now a bit bent on the right; I was not even out of Delhi and already my beautiful Bullet had some bruises.

Despite the bad start to the day, my riding was already showing signs of improvement. Now that I knew where my gears were the ride was a lot smoother. Feeling brave, and bored with going around Connaught Place, I turned off to explore a bit more of Delhi... and ended up getting completely lost in an area full of identical roundabouts. I finally stopped an auto-rickshaw and hired the driver to lead me back to the YMCA.

While riding around the roundabouts I had discovered another particularity of Indian driving: vehicles coming onto a roundabout do not yield to those already on it. This makes for interesting situations in which roundabouts come to a standstill as traffic trying to leave it is blocked by traffic coming onto it.

I decided to set off the next day towards Amritsar.

Chapter 4
Setting off

After countless trips to the toilet – and that was before I even got my first bout of Delhi Belly – numerous checks on the map to learn the first day's route, and tedious repetitions of various Hindi sentences ('Where is...'; 'I don't understand'; 'Turn right/left'; 'Straight on') to try to keep my mind off potential accidents, I finally dozed off at three o'clock in the morning.

As I left Delhi at six o'clock, mist on the ground gave the impression that the buildings were floating on clouds, but the fog became so dense that soon I couldn't see more than 20 metres ahead. Not even out of Delhi and already I had no idea what I was riding into! Fortunately the morning sun eventually burned the fog off and I was able to concentrate on getting to know my motorbike.

For about two thirds of the route, the road – the Grand Trunk Road – was dual carriageway and in good condition. I enjoyed giving the bike full throttle and overtaking overloaded trucks and bullock-driven carts. I even managed to reach up to 120km an hour – at which point the whole bike, and myself, started shaking.

For the final third of the journey the road was single carriageway due to resurfacing work. Riding the bike then became much more difficult, with oncoming truck drivers overtaking each other and playing the Indian version of 'chicken': me as the hapless chicken and the driver as the hungry fox. It took me a while, and a few scary near-misses, to realise I was expected to move out of the way onto the narrow gravel hard shoulder to make room for trucks overtaking each other and seemingly heading straight for me.

The scenery was disappointing: flat agricultural land with the odd ugly motel, military encampments with their obligatory drab prefab tenements, and factories billowing smoke that mingled with the diesel fumes already hanging over the road and burning my eyes and throat. The lack of appeal was probably fortunate, as it allowed me to concentrate on the road ahead of me.

In the afternoon I stopped for a cup of tea at a road-side stall, and tried out one of my newly learned Hindi phrases: 'Chai bina dude' ('tea without milk'). In response I was given tea with marginally less milk. Still, I gulped it down – for the calorific value if not the taste.

In the toilet, I looked at my face in the mirror: even with the visor down on my helmet I could see it was black with dirt, and my bloodshot and exhausted eyes looked back at me wearily. I washed as best as I could and returned to settle my bill.

'Where are you from?' the owner asked as he took my money.

'London, England.'

'London proper?'

'Yes.'

'I am having an uncle living in Manchester. You are very welcome to my country.' He handed back the paper money I had given him. 'The tea is free. You are looking much tired and needing it.'

I finally reached the town of Jalandhar in the late afternoon, and went from hotel to hotel in search of a room. Most of the accommodation had been taken over by Punjabi soldiers sent here to protect the Indian Prime Minister and the British Queen, who were visiting nearby Amritsar. Every time I dismounted I had to be careful not to fall over or drop the bike from exhaustion.

After ten hours on the bike, and a journey of 400km (I never again did such a long day), I was getting worried about where I'd sleep that night. I didn't much like the suggestion from one hotel employee that I ride over to Amritsar, two hours away and in the dark, in search of a hotel room. Eventually, however, the town's top hotel offered me their worst room: a windowless neon-lit room seemingly used for storing linen. Still, it had air-conditioning, room service, a double bed, cable TV – and all the towels and sheets I could wish for.

It was rather embarrassing coming into this posh hotel: I looked like a coal miner with my filthy face. The receptionist continued to call me 'sir' even after hearing my voice, but seamlessly changed to 'madam' when I re-emerged in my elegant punjabi to enjoy a beer in the hotel bar.

Afterwards, I relaxed on the luxurious king-sized bed in my room, eating a stuffed paratha from room service and feeling very proud of myself: I'd managed to get through the first day on the bike with no punctures, no breakdowns and – best of all – no accidents.

Determined not to be one of those helpless females that doesn't know a spark plug from a piston, I pulled the Enfield bike manual out of my bag to learn about the bike. Oops! Maybe I should have read the manual before I set off... It stated that for the first 500km the bike should be ridden at no more than 50km per hour, and that you should stop every hour for ten minutes to let the bike cool down.

The next morning, by way of apology to my two-wheeled companion, I went to the local Enfield dealer to book it in for its 500km service.

The motorcycle shop, near the bus station, was empty.

'Hello! Anybody here?' My words echoed around the room.

No answer.

I walked to the back of the shop, through an open door and into a dark workshop. Three men in oil-covered overalls were working: one was sweeping the cement floor, another was hanging up some spanners while the third was carefully placing bits of bike engines into wooden boxes. All this was happening as if in slow motion.

'Hello,' I said. 'I bought a new Enfield in Delhi and I've come for my first service. Can you do it?'

The sweeper yelled something in Punjabi to someone

outside. A man dressed in a light blue polyester safari suit came in, had a short conversation with the sweeper and walked back out.

The sweeper turned to me and said, 'Servicing possible in one week.'

'A week!' I exclaimed. 'No, I can't wait a week. Can't you do it before?'

He leaned on his broom. 'No. A week. Busy now.'

I looked around and asked, 'All your mechanics?'

'Not possible. All busy,' he insisted.

'Can I speak to the manager, please? Was that the manager before?'

The sweeper shouted in Punjabi again and the manager strolled back in.

'Hello sir. You are having a problem?' he asked.

'Well first of all it's madam!' I corrected him sharply.

'Oh, sorry! But you are very tall and you have very short hair.'

'Yeah, I know... Look, I came from Delhi yesterday with my new Enfield and I need to get its first service. Can you do it today?'

'Madam, I am so very sorry but all our mechanics are busy. We are having an inspection from head office in seven days and we must get ready.'

'You mean to say you can't serve your customers because your boss is coming to inspect your work?' I asked.

He smiled apologetically. 'We must clean the workshop and the office.'

'You're the local Enfield dealer, and you can't serve the owner of a new Enfield because of a visit from head office!?' I slowly crossed my arms; maybe a bit of intimidation would do the trick...

He looked away, shuffled his feet and changed the topic by launching into the usual questions.

'Which is your good name?'

'Which is your country?'

'Which is your profession?'

In a flash of inspiration, I lied: 'Journalist.'

'Oh?' he frowned. 'In a newspaper?'

'Yes, a British paper called *Motorcycle Travel News*,' I added for good measure.

'Oh. Really? You drink some tea? Fanta?'

'Yes, thank you. That's very kind of you. I'd love a Fanta.'

Miraculously, the three cleaners were reassigned as my mechanics and my service was completed in less than two hours. However – perhaps as a punishment for my lie – before I had done 80km I could somehow no longer find my second gear on the Enfield.

~~~~~~~~~~

Upon arrival in Amritsar I met my first fellow Enfield traveller, parked outside the Golden Temple. Yuri, an Israeli sporting a shaved head and a goatee, had just come back from Srinagar in Kashmir.

I was impressed. 'Isn't it dangerous to go there, with all the fighting and the kidnappings?' I asked him.

He sneered. 'You Europeans! You are always afraid of everything. You are too soft. I did not see any fighting. Just a lot of soldiers.'

This made me think: I was only a couple days' riding from Kashmir, with its renowned lush valleys, beautiful mountains and grand old colonial houseboats. In Delhi I'd also met some tourists who'd come back from Kashmir, but they'd gone there by bus and I wasn't sure if the roads were safe to travel solo on a bike. Yuri told me I'd get stopped by the military along the way to check my papers, but nothing more.

It was only after I'd returned from Kashmir that an American pointed out to me that asking an Israeli youth just out of the army whether travelling to a war-torn region was safe may not have been particularly sensible...

Yuri escorted me to the mechanic in Amritsar to attend to my missing second gear. On the way there, he lectured me on the Dos and Don'ts of dealing with mechanics. 'First, you must agree on a price before they start doing the work. It's too late to start bargaining afterwards. Second, you must choose only Enfield mechanics. A lot of scooter mechanics pretend to be Enfield specialists when they see a foreigner. Also, Sikhs are usually the best mechanics.

'Check that they have Enfields in their garage. And if you can find a mechanic with a couple of old Enfields, that's even better. That means he probably uses them for spare parts. Also you must not show them that you don't know about bikes. I tell them I could do the work myself except that I don't have the tools with me.'

'What if you don't know what's wrong with the bike in the first place?' I asked.

'Never, *never*, show them that. I tell them I just don't know the words in English. Also you must never go away when they're working. You must sit with them and watch them. Otherwise they'll pretend they've done something when they haven't – or even steal some of your new parts and replace them with damaged old ones.'

Impressed by his knowledge, I asked, 'How often do you have to visit mechanics?'

'About two or three times a week.'

We found a Sikh mechanic, bargained, looked knowledgeable, and for $1.50 my gear box was dismantled, some bits were oiled, some screws were tightened and – magic! – I regained my second gear.

Later, having changed out of my jeans and into my punjabi, I took a bicycle rickshaw with Yuri to visit the Golden Temple.

As we came to a steep hill, the driver dismounted, pointed to Yuri and said, 'Off, please. Pushing.'

I also moved to get down but the driver indicated that I should remain seated. So Yuri pushed the carriage from behind while the rickshaw driver pushed at the front. I felt rather grand, and a bit silly, especially since both the Indian and Yuri were short and skinny and certainly weighed less than me.

We then ran into a parade of schoolchildren, dancing troupes, men on horseback and musical bands on their way to the Temple to celebrate the anniversary of the birth of the Sikhs' fourth Guru.

The courtyard in the Golden Temple was crowded with worshippers: the men in yellow, red, pink and blue turbans, and the women in equally colourful punjabis. With its cool white marble, its shimmering pond and the clean majestic lines of its buildings, the temple was a haven from the dusty, crowded and noisy city outside its walls.

In one of the kiosks I made a contribution to the upkeep of the temple by buying some prassad – a sweet and sticky cake. The attendants took back half of it to distribute to the pilgrims as they left the temple, and with the other half I could do as I pleased.

After only one bite I knew I'd have to dispose of it; it was so sweet my teeth ached.

I walked up to the sacred pond and dropped it in the water. Almost immediately, scores of big fat fish came up to the surface and devoured it like hungry piranhas. Judging by the size of those fish, I suspect they'd been fed prassad many times before.

The pilgrims in the temple were extremely friendly – especially the women, who gave me big smiles. After being mistaken for a man for the past few days, it was nice to feel like a woman again.

Later, I went to the nearby Jallianwala Bagh – a memorial park that commemorates the hundreds of Indian demonstrators killed by the British there in 1919. I sat on a low wall with some women, who taught me how to say hello in Punjabi. I think it went something like 'satshri akal'.

While I sat surrounded by the women, an imposing man with a large purple turban and an enormous mutton chop moustache approached us. In good English, he asked me where I came from.

Hesitating, I replied, 'England.'

'Ah, the Britishers did many bad things here.' He pointed to the bullet-riddled walls. 'Many people were killed here by your people.'

Embarrassed, I answered, 'Yes I know. It was a very bad thing.'

'Your Queen Elizabeth was here two days ago to visit Amritsar,' he added.

I looked down at my feet. 'Yes, I know.'

'She didn't say sorry for the massacre,' he insisted.

The English language newspapers that day had been full of indignant editorials criticising the lack of official British apology.

I mumbled, 'Yes, I did read about it. I'm sorry about that.'

He shrugged. 'Thank you, but it is your Queen who should apologise.'

This was the only occasion in my year-long trip that I encountered any bad feelings towards the British.

The next day I said goodbye to Yuri and got back on my bike to head towards Kashmir. On my way out of Amritsar I got lost and ended up doing a two-hour detour on very small country lanes, passing numerous herds of cattle as they meandered aimlessly in the middle of the road. I assumed they belonged to somebody but there was no herder in sight.

The cows in India are quite something: they've obviously figured out they're sacred to Hindus and they just wander along the roads. Sometimes they even sit down in the middle of the street or on a busy roundabout – especially if there's something edible to nibble on.

I finally rejoined the main road after stopping a dozen times to ask for directions. It should have been simple since I wanted the road to a large city called Jammu, but somehow I managed to mispronounce it.

I'd pull up to a farmer walking along, point to the road and ask, 'Jammu?'

Blank stare.

'Jammu', I'd repeat.

'Sorry, no English.' He'd walk away.

The next person, the same problem.

As far as I can figure it out, it's simply pronounced as it's written, but obviously my accent must have been very bad, since this scenario was repeated again and again.

Finally I pulled up to a portly man, dressed in immaculate white tunic and trousers, waiting at a junction.

'Jammu?'

Blank look.

I pulled out my map and pointed to the town.

'Ah! Jammu!' he exclaimed. And then added in English, 'You must take this road on the right.'

I swear, to me, it sounded just the way I'd said it.

Once back on the main road, the wind picked up, the sky got very dark and a few minutes later it started to pour. And I mean *really* pour. The monsoon had officially ended the previous month, but this was not your usual afternoon rain shower. I put on my waterproofs – which turned out not to be so waterproof – over my already wet trousers.

Over the next six hours I averaged a speed of 25km per hour. In places, the road disappeared into murky ponds, and eventually I had to stop when a fast-flowing river swallowed up the road.

I pulled off to the side alongside a dozen scooters and a couple cars that were surveying the water rushing in front of us. Trucks and buses were just going through with little trouble and big splashes. For us, of course, it was rather different. Eventually one of the scooter riders decided to go ahead; I'm embarrassed to say that I, on my big 500cc motorbike, was hesitant.

The rider made it through to the other side, even though at one point both his wheels were completely submerged. Shamed, I kick-started my bike and followed him. It wasn't too bad, except that my boots filled up with muddy water because – unlike the scooter rider – I hadn't dared to lift my feet off the footrests.

My destination was still another couple of hours away,

but first I had to make a toilet stop. I found a roadside café, ordered a black tea (which again came with milk) and asked for the toilet. After much sign language it became evident that the 'toilet' was out there, in the open. Not willing to go in full view of the road, I drank my tea and rode another half hour before coming to a more upmarket place with a toilet.

Eventually I reached Jammu. I checked into a simple guesthouse where I discovered that not only all the clothes I was wearing were wet, but so were those in my luggage since I'd not had the foresight to put my gear in plastic bags.

Feeling a bit down and lonely, I curled up under the bed covers with a glass of warming Scotch.

The next morning, as I was loading up my bike in the hotel courtyard, a friend of the hotel manager – or so he said – approached me.

'Are you going to Kashmir?' he asked.

'Yes.'

'Where will you be staying? In Srinagar? My family has a beautiful hotel. You will like it very much there.'

'That's nice.'

'Why don't you book it with me. I make sure you have the best room.'

I continued securing my luggage. 'No, thank you. I'll find one when I get there.'

'But there are many bad hotels. We have a beautiful houseboat. Look.'

He produced a folder with faded polaroids and dozens of letters from previous guests praising the accommodation, the food and the service. The letters were fifteen years old.

'Very nice,' I said as I handed them back to him. 'But I prefer to find my own place when I get there.'

'I can give you a very good price. You see, the usual price is 2,000 rupees, but because the tourists are very few you can have it for 600 rupees.'

'I'm sure it's a very good price, but I'd prefer to get

my own hotel there.'

'But there are many dishonest people in Srinagar,' he insisted. 'They will tell you they have a beautiful hotel, but when you get there you'll find that the boat is old and dirty.'

'I'm sure some people are bad,' I said, 'but I promise you I'll inspect the houseboat before I accept. Now really, I must go. It's a long journey.'

I climbed onto my bike, put on my helmet and started the engine. Still he wouldn't move out of my way. He took hold of my wrist.

I switched off the engine. 'Look! I'm not going to book anything from here. Give me your hotel card and I'll look at it when I get there. Now, I'm going.'

'Do you promise to go there first?'

'Yes' I lied. 'Now can I go?'

He gave me a handful of cards and started explaining how I could find his brother's houseboat. Finally he let me leave and I rode to the petrol station to fill up for the journey. The attendant went into the hut to bring me my change, and came back with a brochure for another houseboat.

He was barely into his routine of 'the usual price is 2,500 rupees but I can make you a special price of 500 rupees,' when I thanked him and pulled away.

I'd been warned that the Kashmiri tourist industry was desperate for business, but I didn't expect the hard-sell to start two day's riding away from Srinagar.

~~~~~~~~~~

The initial journey up towards the Kashmir Valley was lovely: I climbed up relatively quiet roads and the scenery became progressively greener and more forested. However, after three hours I hit a patch of road under construction. This is where a trail bike would have been useful. And to make matters worse, I got stuck in a convoy of trucks and military jeeps.

So there I was, riding through beautiful mountains... and all I could see were the backs of dusty trucks and their trails of black diesel fumes. This went on for a couple of hours, even though I was slowly overtaking whenever I had the courage to ride on the other side of the road, ready to dart back in at the first sound of a big truck thundering down in the opposite direction.

Eventually the convoys – there was one in each direction by this point – came to a complete stop. The trucks just sat there, having thankfully turned off their engines.

And then the fun started.

There are few things more satisfying than weaving your bike in and out of almost four kilometres of stationary traffic.

To come back to the rules of Indian driving: that day, as I manoeuvred my bike between vehicles, I noticed that very few of them had side mirrors. When I'd bought my bike, the dealer had asked me if I wanted mirrors fitted and, of course, I said yes. Now I know that in fact they impede your ability to get through tight spaces, and since you're focusing so much on what's in front of you, there isn't any time to keep an eye on what's behind anyway. Instead people use their horns to warn traffic ahead of their presence. You have to assume those behind you know you're there, and that they'll react appropriately to your manoeuvres.

By this time, both myself and the bike looked much more the part: the bike had acquired a respectable coat of dust and dried mud, and quite a few scratches on the tank from the zip of my leather jacket, while I had acquired a respectable set of muscles on my arms and shoulders.

I was also very much enjoying the riding – and showed my enjoyment by sporadically screaming into my helmet, '*Yeah! I love this! This is great!*'

Worryingly, I also caught myself exclaiming, '*This is so easy!*' as I weaved my bike between trucks, swerved around a large pothole or lifted my legs up in a double

Kung Fu kick while I accelerated through a giant puddle. A week on the roads and I'd become an expert rider.

Chapter 5
A few problems in Kashmir

This was the life: sitting on a houseboat that oozed faded grandeur while looking out at the white water lilies on a still lake, and the Kashmiri mountains beyond. It would've been be perfect if it weren't for the constant stream of vendors on little boats who moored up to my veranda and tried to peddle their goods – chocolates, soft drinks, cigarettes, toilet paper, shampoo, jewellery, Kashmiri shawls and carpets.

Finding a place to stay in Srinagar had been easy since there were more than two thousand houseboats to choose from and probably less than a hundred tourists. I had the entire eight-bedroomed boat to myself, and the full attention of the owner.

The houseboats were an ingenious introduction to the region by the British during the Raj period. They'd come to the cooler climes of Kashmir during the summer, but were unable to build homes there because the local government forbade them from owning land. To get around this they simply built their summer homes on the lake.

The owner of my houseboat told me that when he was a child, his grandfather used to be a servant for an English colonel and his family. He said the English were very strict about tidiness, noise and the 'proper' way of doing things. His grandfather used to wait on them wearing a white starched uniform with a napkin over his forearm, and the kitchen was kept on a separate boat half a kilometre away so that the smells and the clanking of pans wouldn't disturb the family.

The owner told me that once, when he was four years old, he fell down on one of the planks connecting the various boats and hurt his knee. He started howling and ran towards his mother, at which point the colonel emerged from his houseboat, caught the little boy by the arm and growled at him to be quiet. He recounted that the fear of this big English man with the small moustache silenced him on the spot.

~~~~~~~~~~~

One problem with staying on the houseboat was finding a place for my motorbike. For security reasons, the military authorities decreed that no vehicle should be left unattended on the road anywhere in the city, and my houseboat owner explained that security was even tighter than usual because the Prime Minister was about to come for an inspection. Along the boulevard by the lake, military jeeps drove up and down and soldiers stood guard every 50 metres. I found a home owner who stored my bike in his courtyard for a small fee.

On my second day there I rode to the old part of Srinagar to visit the Jama Masjid mosque, famous for its three hundred wooden pillars, originally built in 1385 and rebuilt after a fire in 1674. The road outside the mosque was very busy and noisy, but as soon as I walked through the large wooden gate the noises became muffled and gradually died out completely once I got deep into the building. A few men were praying, softly reciting verses from the Koran. Trying to be as unobtrusive as possible, I meandered around the large open area, enjoying the calm beauty and the peaceful atmosphere.

Once back out of the mosque, as I was putting my boots back on, a Kashmiri man in his late twenties, wearing jeans and a black leather jacket, approached me.

He spoke in an angry tone: 'You Westerners all think bad things about Muslims! You think we are not good people. You blame us for everything bad in the world.'

'I don't think that,' I said in my defence.

'All Westerners think bad things about Islam. I know. I listen to your radio. It's full of propaganda against

Muslims. Always talking about Muslim fundamentalists, Muslim fanatics, Muslim terrorists. Your press wants the world to think that the Kashmiri problem is a religious problem. It's not.'

'Actually, I don't know much about the political problems of Kashmir,' I said, as I finished lacing up my boots.

He pointed to a small tea shop across the road. 'Have some tea with me and I will explain it to you.'

He was telling me, not asking me.

I looked around. We were standing outside the mosque in a busy road with a street market, and many people were looking at us.

I hesitated. 'What about my bike? Can I leave it parked here?'

He took my arm. 'Don't worry, everybody knows me here. Nobody will dare touch your bike now.'

If that was supposed to reassure me, it didn't. Why would everybody here know him? And why should they be afraid of him?

We entered the tea shop, my host said a few words in the local language and two young men vacated a table for us. They, and the other patrons, sat by the opposite wall, watching and listening to us. My companion was obviously influential.

Two cups of tea, slightly sweetened, milk-free and flavoured with cinnamon, were placed in front of us. Delicious.

My host was very fluent in English. He argued that Kashmir, with its majority Muslim population, should have been incorporated into Pakistan at the time of Partition of India in 1947, since that had been the main criteria for joining one or the other nation. However, he said, the ruler of Kashmir – a Hindu – had decided to join India despite the wishes of the majority, and since then Kashmiris have been trying to expel the Indian army from their territory.

I asked him if Kashmiris still wanted to be part of

Pakistan. He lowered his voice and answered, 'No, we want to be independent.'

Then he looked at his watch and said, 'I have to leave. I am very busy. Goodbye.'

Dismissed, I got back on my bike and rode back to the houseboat, where I got a bollocking from the owner.

'You should not go to the mosque!'

'Why?'

'Did you see any soldiers there?' he asked.

'No.'

'That's right!' he shouted. 'That's because it's too dangerous for the army – and for tourists. There is much fighting in that part of Srinagar. The Kashmiri resistance is very strong there. The people you met there are dangerous. You are very lucky and very foolish!'

In fact, according to him, most of old Srinagar was too dangerous and out of bounds to me. He suggested instead that I take a two-day motorbike trip up the Sindh Valley to the village of Sonamarg.

Chastened, I followed his advice, and the next day set off on a route that quickly deteriorated from a tarmacked road with the odd pot-hole to a rocky track with the odd bit of tarmac.

After overtaking my twentieth military truck – presumably on its way to the battlefields with Pakistan – I got a puncture. I would have preferred to get my first puncture in a more peaceful area of India, but since there was an armed Indian sentinel on the top of the hill above me, at least I probably didn't have to worry about being kidnapped... I hoped.

I waved down a civilian truck and asked the driver if he could get me help in Kangan, the nearest village, 12km away. While I waited, I examined my back tyre for the cause of the puncture, but couldn't find anything embedded. It must've been one of the many sharp rocks on this excuse for a road.

Strangely, I wasn't afraid at all. And yet when I look back on this, I'm struck by my stupidity. Here I was, stuck on my own near a violent battle zone with a simple puncture I couldn't repair on my own.

As I sat under an overcast sky that was threatening snow, and watched the Indian soldier watching me, an old bearded man walked up the road. He wore a dirty yellow turban and was wrapped in a blanket decorated with bright geometric shapes.

'Namaste,' I smiled.

He looked at me but only nodded.

He slowly walked up to my bike and examined it carefully while I sat with my luggage spread out around me.

'You speak English?' I asked.

The old man looked up at me, but again did not answer. He then walked up to where I was sitting, crouched down to my level and studied my helmet on the ground.

'You want to see my helmet?' I asked, as I handed it over to him.

He put down his walking stick and gently took my helmet. He examined it from all angles, lifted up the visor and handed it back without a word. He then shook my hand, picked up his stick and slowly walked off back down the road.

After a two-hour wait, a truck came down the valley and deposited two men who introduced themselves as my rescuers.

'We are coming to bring your puncture to Kangan,' the darker-skinned of the two said.

They quickly took off the back wheel, helped me with my luggage, and stopped the first vehicle – another truck – that came down the mountain; we all piled in next to the driver and half an hour later we were at the puncture shop.

While watching them repair my inner tube, I struck up a conversation with the two men. The tall fair one, who was Kashmiri, didn't speak any English; while the other, who was of a slighter build and darker complexion, came from Karnataka – a state far down in the south of India –

and spoke very good English.

He started with the usual questions: 'Which is your mother country?', 'What is your good name?', 'Are you married?' and 'How old are you?' When I told him I was 33 he exclaimed, 'But you should be married by now and have children!'

'How many children do you have?' I asked.

'Two girls. They live with my wife in Karnataka. I work here most of the year and spend the winter with them.'

'What is your job?'

'I work on the roads. I operate a bulldozer here. My job is clearing the rocks that are falling on the roads.'

'So why did you come with the puncture wallah to help me?'

'Today I do not work. I came to the village to buy meat and spoke to the truck driver who came to say there was a foreigner who needed help. The puncture man does not speak English so I came with him.'

I thanked him.

'Do you like working here?'

'Yes Kashmir is very beautiful, but there is much fighting.'

'Does it make you afraid?'

He answered. 'No. I am Christian. The Kashmir people have no problems with Christians. It is with the Hindus they have problems.'

Eight months later, 35 road workers, many of them Christians, were ambushed and killed by Kashmiri militants.

After we'd finished at the puncture repair shop we hailed a bus to return to the bike.

Carrying my wheel and helmet, I tried to board the bus, but there wasn't enough room inside. The conductor pointed to the roof. 'Bus full. Too much people inside. You climb on the roof.'

I hesitated and he got impatient, took the motorcycle wheel from my hands and threw it up to the roof where a group of men, already installed there, caught it. My companions – the Kashmiri and the Karnataka man – quickly climbed on and I followed up the ladder with my helmet through my arm. The bus took off before I reached the top. As it lurched violently from side to side alongside a ravine, I inched my way up the ladder until the men on the roof could haul me up. They cleared a patch in the middle of the group for me to sit, and I held onto my two companions. Neither of them complained, although I'm sure I must've cut off the circulation in their arms. If I'd had the courage to let go just for one instant, I would've put my helmet on for protection. The view was probably beautiful from this vantage point but I kept my eyes closed for most of the way.

After the puncture incident, which took a total of five hours to deal with, I was very happy to be back on the bike. For the rest of the ride up to Sonamarg I admired the mountains shrouded in wisps of cloud, and although it rained at times I also saw silvery rays of sunshine breaking through, and countless rainbows. At one point I rode along a stream that was fluorescent blue, with the trees in full autumn colours. This is the scenery that made Kashmir world-famous.

~~~~~~~~~~~~~

The room I rented in Sonamarg consisted simply of four walls and a sheet of corrugated iron for a roof. My mattress was made out of blankets laid out on the wooden floor, where I spent the first evening sitting, all wrapped up, with a small clay pot filled with burning coal placed between my legs to keep me warm. The people here called it a 'Winter Wife'. I would have liked a whole harem.

The next day I sat at a table in the sun, outside my hut, wearing all my motorcycle gear and a filthy blanket around my shoulders, drinking tea and reading Jack Kerouac's *On the Road*.

This little village's main reason for being, apart from

providing summer grazing, is to offer lunch to passing travellers. As the lunch hour approached, the workers in the single row of roadside cafés went into a frenzy of activity, getting the rice, lentils and chapatis ready.

I watched the buses and trucks pull in. The buses carried mainly Tibetan passengers from Ladakh, while the trucks carried military personnel and road workers leaving the region before winter. Not one tourist.

The road to Leh in Ladakh is 350km long and often unpaved. There's no point in sealing it because every year snow avalanches and landslides take off big chunks of it. In a good year it stays open for seven months, and the road workers' job is to try and smooth it out as much as possible. This means mainly clearing landslides with a bulldozer, if they can get one there, or by hand and dynamite, and filling up potholes. On my way up to Sonamarg I'd seen workers filling up a large crater in the road: first they threw in small boulders almost to the top, and then they switched to smaller rocks. It made for a bumpy crossing, but it worked.

After the midday rush, Rafiq, the manager of the place I was staying in, sat down with me for a cup of tea. He was in his early twenties, very slim, and had striking green eyes.

As we watched the workers go back to their trucks, I asked him, 'How much do they get paid?'

'It depends on the work, but some of them get 100 rupees a day.'

Less than three dollars a day.

'Is that a good wage?' I asked.

'Yes. They are poor people and they come from far for work. They come from Nepal, Bihar and Rajasthan.' He added. 'Now they go home for the winter.'

I could see two policemen talking to the truck drivers and I asked Rafiq what was going on.

'They are checking that the driver has the right papers for the workers. If they don't they must pay 1,000 rupees.'

'That's a lot!' I exclaimed.

'Yes. And everybody knows that the policeman steals it. Even if you have the papers you must still pay him 30 rupees.'

We continued to watch them, and although I had no reason to doubt what Rafiq had told me, I couldn't see any resentment on anyone's faces. On the contrary, the policemen and the truck drivers seemed to be getting along very well, joking and laughing.

He poured me another cup of tea.

'You speak very good English,' I remarked. 'How did you learn it?'

'I am a university student in Srinagar. The classes are in English.'

'So you don't usually work here?'

'I stay here only for a few days at a time. Sometimes my brother comes here, sometimes me, sometimes my father. Tonight my father is coming and I will go back to Srinagar.'

'How will you go back?' I asked.

'Maybe...' he grinned, 'you will take me back?'

I laughed. 'I don't have much experience riding with a passenger. In fact I've never done it.'

'No problem, it is easy. I am sure you can do it,' he answered.

I smiled. 'If you have so much confidence in me, I have no choice but to say yes.'

In the morning, after another very cold night with the temperature going down to minus seven degrees centigrade, I couldn't start the bike. I tried again and again, but all I got in response were a few calf-bruising revenges from the kick-start as it swung back to its initial position.

Rafiq suggested trying a downhill start. Fine, but the only problem was I didn't know how to do that. He, who had never ridden a bike, or driven a car, explained that I needed to get into first gear and slowly release the clutch once the bike was travelling at a reasonable speed. (I later learned from experience that this works much better if the bike's in third gear.)

Surprisingly, the ride with Rafiq on the back of the bike turned out to be quite fun. I was a bit wobbly at the beginning, but once I put it out of my mind that I was carrying a helmet-less passenger, it got much easier.

As we said goodbye in front of his house in Srinigar, Rafiq said, 'Thank you for taking me. You are a very safe and careful motorcycle driver.'

I think this meant I'd ridden too slow for his liking; it had taken us three hours to cover the 85km to Srinagar. But then the local bus would have taken six hours, as it stops at almost every bend to drop off and pick up passengers.

~~~~~~~~~~~

Three days later I left Srinagar for Patni Top, which was 200km away. While filling up for the journey I managed to open up my oil gauge for the first time, and discovered I needed a top-up. My manual specified that I should use '20/50W' oil; I had no idea what that meant, but despite going to five different petrol stations in search of it I could only find 20/40W oil. I was about to buy it, with some misgivings, when a motorist advised me that a shop in the town centre sold 20/50W oil.

However, since the shops in India don't open until 10am, I parked outside to wait. As soon as I dismounted, an Indian soldier came up to me and ordered me to move off. It was still only 9am, so I decided to ride around the commercial centre. I obviously aroused suspicion: twice I was pulled over and had my papers and luggage checked by the army – in search of explosives, I presume.

It was quite late by the time I finally left Srinagar to begin my trip out of Kashmir. I tried to catch up on lost time and overtook many trucks and buses. At one point, however, I almost fell into a ravine when I overtook a truck at the same time as it was overtaking another. I confused the signal for 'It's safe to overtake now, as long as you do it in the next two seconds' (a wave of the driver's hand out of the window from back to front) with the signal for 'Don't do it unless you want to add to the collection of rusted vehicles at the bottom of the mountain' (the driver sticks out his hand with the index finger pointing down).

Even the truck driver looked frightened when I glanced back at him.

~~~~~~~~~~

After spending a night in Patni Top, I set off the next morning. A few hours into the journey, I pulled into a lay-by overlooking the beautiful mountains and met an Australian couple travelling on an Enfield 500, also admiring the view.

The man, Greg, was smoking hash and offered me a puff.

'No thanks,' I said, 'I find it hard enough to ride when I've *got* all my faculties.'

'I find it relaxes me, and this way I make sure I don't ride too quickly,' he responded. 'You're coming from Srinagar?'

They too had been there, via Ladakh.

'What's Ladakh like?' I asked.

Jess, a petite redhead in her thirties, answered. 'Amazing. Beautiful mountains, Buddhist monasteries, really friendly people. But it's almost November and the road's closed for the winter. You can't get there now until next summer. If you're still in India then, you really should go.'

They were going in the same direction as me, and we decided to ride together. In view of Greg's dope-smoking, I decided to stay well behind their bike.

We were going up a hill and round a curve when suddenly I saw a truck in front of me careering down in the middle of the road. If I'd hugged the curve as I should have, it would have been a near miss. Instead I collided with the side of the truck.

I'd like to say I took some evasive action, but I didn't. It seemed to happen in slow motion – although not slow enough for me to swerve.

I was lying in the middle of the road with my right leg trapped under the bike when the driver of the truck ran out of his car, shouting, 'Crazy, crazy tourist! Too fast. Wrong side of the road.'

I was too stunned to respond.

He continued his tirade and I stayed under the bike until my Australian companions lifted it off me and pushed it to the side of the road. I slowly got up; I didn't feel too bad and obviously nothing was broken.

I sat by the roadside saying little, while the truck driver started up the offensive again, and my newly acquired Australian friends took up my defence.

'You know that in India cars drive on the left?' the truck driver asked aggressively.

'Very funny,' Jess responded. 'So how come you were driving on the right?'

'Does she have a motorcycle licence?'

'Do you have a truck driving licence?'

'How long has she been riding a motorbike?'

Oh, no! Better not answer that one, I thought. I changed the subject. 'We need to get the police for the insurance claim.'

Everyone looked at me, puzzled.

'My insurance will pay for the repairs to the bike, but first I must get a police report.'

'How much to repair the bike?' the truck driver asked.

'I'm not sure. Maybe more than 3,000 rupees.' (Less than $90.)

He looked shocked – and so did Jess and Greg – at the mention of what I later found out was a ridiculously large amount of money.

We decided to stop all this arguing for now and inspect the damage. Me: a ripped leather jacket, a grazed elbow, a bruised knee and a slightly sprained ankle. The bike: a bent leg frame and foot rest, broken clutch and brake bracket, a smashed headlight, side indicator and mirror.

Greg and the truck driver decided they could repair the most crucial elements and get the motorcycle back on the road. As the two men replaced the brackets with the spares Greg carried, Jess whispered to me, 'We've had to change our front forks a month ago, and that only cost 2,000 rupees. Your repairs will cost a lot less.'

The work on the bike went very well and the whole atmosphere improved.

The driver offered me some water and said, 'I am a poor man with much children... You will not call the police?'

Feeling rather foolish that I'd ever mentioned the police, I answered, 'No. There's no point in calling the police. And I don't want money from you. It's very kind of you to repair my bike.'

The two men managed to get my bike going again, and I parted company with the Australian couple to go in search of a mechanic for further repairs.

A man on a scooter showed me the way to the nearest town. As he said goodbye, he warned me, 'Quiet roads like this are more dangerous than busy ones because the truck drivers think there is nobody else on the road. They drive in the middle of the road, or even on the other side if the condition of the road is better there.'

Looking back, I couldn't really say who was responsible for the accident. Was I really in my lane? ('Lane' being a rather generous word.) I'm just grateful the Australian couple were there to help and the truck driver didn't just drive on. The bill at the mechanics came to 300 rupees ($9): a pretty cheap lesson.

The next 80km to the nearest sizeable town – Pathankot – felt very long as I kept going over the accident. Could I have avoided it? Would I have any more accidents? What if the next accident turned out to be much more serious? Was I foolish in thinking I could learn to ride well enough to go on such a trip?

As the adrenaline started ebbing away, the pain in my ankle increased. It was my gear-changing foot. Eventually I had to do most of the journey in fourth gear, and when I really had no choice but to change down, I'd stop the bike, bend over and change the gears with my hands. Thankfully the bike was not heavily loaded and I found it still had quite a bit of pull in fourth gear – even if I was going quite slowly.

That evening, lying on my bed with a pack of ice around my ankle, I continued thinking about the day's events. This was the closest I'd been to death and it made me realise how easy it is to die. A split second of inattention and that's it: one moment you're there, the next you're not. I thought, Okay, so it didn't happen today, but I will die one day. Maybe in fifty years, but maybe tomorrow. Death isn't just something that happens to other people; it's just a question of time.

I knew that before, of course, but I'd managed to convince myself that because it'd be a long time coming, I could pretend it never would.

~~~~~~~~~~~

The next day, feeling slightly stiff, I rode out to Dalhousie – a town 100km away. The route followed some beautiful mountain roads. I kept a very low speed and stayed close to the curve, reminding myself of what Greg had advised me: 'Imagine that around every bend there's a big fridge freezer standing in the middle of the road.'

Dalhousie, my stop for the night, was a hill resort at an altitude of 2,000 metres. Very popular with Indian tourists, it used to be a place where the British would go to escape the heat of the Delhi summers. At the time of year I was there, however, it could get quite cold.

My hotel was built 80 years ago by the English, and had clearly not been repainted since then.

I was in my room when Jess and Greg, my two Australians friends, knocked on the door.

'Hey stranger! We saw your bike outside. Jess recognised it was yours because of the dents. How are you feeling? The bruises changed to a nice green colour yet?'

I proudly displayed my multi-coloured injuries, and we passed the day sitting in my hotel room overlooking the rain-filled valley, wrapped up in blankets, drinking coffee (Jess), smoking pot (Greg) and sipping Scotch (me).

I spent the next two days with them and then we rode out together to the nearby town of Chamba. We went through pine-covered mountains and alongside deep ravines. I rode very slowly and saw fridge freezers everywhere.

In Chamba, at breakfast on my own, I met a young English woman who was taking a year out before going off to university.

Whilst eating my stuffed paratha, I asked, 'What made you decide to travel?'

'Well, the careers advisor said employers prefer people who've taken a year off. It means you're more mature – and less likely to do it again, since you've got the travelling bug out of your system. Also,' she took a bite from her omelette, 'I don't feel ready to settle down yet. I want to do something for myself first. And besides, I'll have all the time later to stay put. Three years of studying... then work... then, I suppose, before you know it, mortgages, husband and kids!' She laughed. 'Did you take a year off after school?'

'No, I didn't.'

'Is that why you're doing it now?'

'Maybe. I don't know.'

'Well, I think what you're doing is really brave,' she said.

'What do you mean?'

God, I hope she's not making reference to me being a bit long in the tooth. To an 18-year-old I must seem really old.

'Well, you know, a woman on a motorcycle on her own, travelling in India.'

I shrugged modestly, putting on my best oh-it's-no-big-deal smile. 'It's not really that bad.'

'Well I think it's brave. I don't know many people who would do this.'

Oh, yes. Give me more. I love it.

Actually, as much as I enjoyed the compliment, I also found this bravery theme a bit unsettling. Bravery implies danger; and if I started believing it, I'd lose what confidence I'd managed to build up. Besides, in truth, travelling by bus in the Indian mountains is, in my opinion, considerably braver: I'd read in the papers that two days previously, not very far from Chamba, a bus had overturned into a river, killing 40 people. It didn't surprise me, since the roads in the area are very narrow and winding, and the buses travel much too fast.

In any case, what's scary for one person isn't necessarily scary for another. For me, so far fear had consisted of having to sing on stage at summer camp when I was ten, or deciding to leave an unhappy marriage four years previously – or even handing in my resignation before coming on this trip.

In those instances I would agree that I was being brave. But since I'm not terrified of riding my motorbike, then it can't be bravery.

On my way out of Chamba, after I'd said goodbye to my Australian friends, I passed the body of a man lying on the road alongside bits of shattered windscreen. Somebody was leaning over him.

I wasn't brave enough to stop.

Chapter 6
Into the swing in Himachal Pradesh

Dharamsala, the seat of the Tibetan government-in-exile, is home to a large population of Tibetan refugees, many of whom walked for days across the High Himalayas to escape from Chinese rule. They come here to be near their spiritual leader, the Dalai Lama, and often to further their religious studies in a monastery or a nunnery.

As I walked in the small streets of the town, among the Tibetan faces I also spotted quite a few young Westerners with the shaved heads and maroon robes of Buddhist monks.

In the terraced gardens of one the monasteries, a young American monk was showing his middle-aged parents around. I assumed they'd come to visit their son's new home, and I wondered if they were also hoping to convince him to return to the States.

The young man had baby-blue eyes and a healthy pink complexion, and though he barely looked out of his teens, he seemed to have a confidence beyond his years.

'Now you see, Dad,' he explained, pointing to a group of fluttering flags, 'they've planted the prayer flags here because there's a lot of wind. That way the wind can carry messages of peace to far-away places.'

His father, who looked rather uncomfortable in a brand new outfit that screamed Timberland from head to toe, answered in an absent-minded tone, 'Hmmm... Yes? That's interesting.'

His mother, who was also in new hiking clothes, was much more impressed. 'Oh! I think that's just so sweet!' She smiled as she touched the blue cloth of one of the flags.

She then noticed a small group of young Tibetans boys, sitting on a blanket on the ground and reading from

Buddhist scripture books.

'Oh! Look at those little boys!' she exclaimed. 'Aren't they just beautiful! Are they trainee monks too?' she asked her son.

Instead, her husband answered. 'Don't ask stupid questions, Marcia. Why do you think they're dressed like Jeff? Of *course* they are.'

Other permanent Western residents in Dharamsala included some throwbacks to the sixties, who spent their time smoking pot and going on free residential meditation courses. Their middle-class parents too, I imagined, had probably once come to try and convince them to go home.

I saw one Westerner wearing the loincloth and dreadlocks of a saddhu – a wandering Hindu pilgrim. Judging by the length of his beard and hair, he must have undergone his conversion many years before. It was later explained to me by an Indian that Hindus tend to look down on such converts, because most believe you can only be *born* a Hindu: it's not possible to *become* one. Therefore Westerners who dress themselves as saddhus risk being accused of mocking Hinduism.

Besides the spiritual activities, there was little to do in Dharamsala but sample the many different restaurants that served Western dishes – or their local versions: pizzas with bases made out of chapati bread, chilli con carne with lentils instead of beans, or spaghetti alla carbonara made from Chinese noodles, curd and greasy bits of pork.

Dharamsala also had the attraction of a couple of cafés with computers linked up to the internet, and I enjoyed receiving and sending e-mails. I did wonder why the messages from Matthew, my boyfriend in London, seemed to be limited mainly to the weather and work. Was he having doubts about our relationship, I thought, or should I just put it down to his usual lawyerly reticence?

I considered going on a Buddhist retreat here – out of curiosity more than anything else – but the idea of not being allowed to talk for 10 days put me off...

Feeling I should at least make some effort to

understand a bit more about Buddhism, I found a book called *Introduction to Buddhism* in one of the second-hand bookshops. Even though, of course, I only got a very superficial look into the philosophy, I did like its emphasis on finding your peace within yourself rather than seeking some outside saviour. Another thing that seems to be emphasised in Buddhism is the importance of logical reasoning to reach the truth. How the belief in reincarnation fits into this, however, escapes me. But what most impressed me about the philosophy was the acceptance that everything is temporary – unhappiness as much as happiness – which helped explain the look of serenity on the faces of Buddhist monks.

During my stay, the Dalai Lama had his monthly 'meet the people' session. Since I have very little patience, I couldn't see myself standing in line for three hours waiting for my turn to shake hands with him. So instead I enjoyed a stroll around the near-deserted town while hundreds of people queued up at his residence.

While walking in the narrow alleyways I met a Yorkshireman in his fifties. He lived in Dharamsala for six months in every year, and was about to move down south to Goa for the winter. He owned three motorbikes: two Enfields for the mountains and a BSA for Goa.

'What do you ride in London?' he asked me.

Usually I'd lie and say a Kawasaki GT550 – the only big bike name that I knew.

'A Vespa,' I answered this time, almost defiantly.

Surprisingly, he approved. 'Ah, great little scooters. I had a Lambretta myself in Leeds.' He continued, 'So how's your Enfield holding up to the mountains? I see your front fork suspension is leaking, and... bleeding heck! When was the last time you tightened your chain?'

'Er... a while.'

'You don't know how to do it, do you?' he laughed. 'Come on, I'll show you.'

He taught me how to tighten the chain as well as how to adjust the brakes, which had been getting even worse.

He also discovered that the very heavy toolkit that the dealer had given me when I bought the bike was all wrong: all the spanners were imperial, whilst most of the nuts and bolts on the Enfield 500 were metric.

~~~~~~~~~~~

The problem of naming my bike had been troubling me. Yuri, the Israeli who'd told me about Kashmir, had named his bike Priscilla Queen of the Mountains. Mine obviously needed a male name. I toyed with the idea of Popeye, because despite an apparently inefficient engine it was able to withstand knocks and still keep going. But eventually, because I have a dirty mind – and an unoriginal one at that – and the engine made a distinctive thumping sound, I settled on Big Thumper.

On a similar theme, one day I read the matrimonial ads in one of the English-language newspapers. Most seemed to be from men looking for beautiful brides from good families. The men declared their age, their height and their salary. The highest salary I saw was 10,000 rupees per month, which comes to just under $300. In most cases the men also indicated their caste, but I did see some ads where caste was stated as less important than education and family background. There were also a couple of ads from the families of men living in the United States who would be visiting India; these families wanted to show the young men a portfolio of potential brides.

Another article in the paper reported on a recent car bomb in the centre of Srinagar in Kashmir that had killed nine people. I now understood why I wasn't allowed to park my bike in the town. The newspaper quoted a minister as saying, 'The recent spate of explosions does not indicate a resurgence of terrorist activities.' What *does* it indicate, then? An imminent peace treaty?

On a lighter note, I also read in the paper that it had just become compulsory in Delhi for both bike riders and their passengers to wear helmets. Sikh men and women were exempt from this rule on religious grounds. Sikh men could be easily identified from their large turbans, but the police would have more difficulty identifying Sikh women, who dress in a less distinctive fashion.

A journalist asked a Sikh representative, 'How will the police recognise Sikh women?'

The official answered, 'The police will recognise a Sikh woman because she'll be riding behind a Sikh man.'

(Neither, it seems, was the possibility of a woman riding her own motorbike even considered by the advertisers at Enfield: a brochure I picked up from the dealership in Jalandhar featured a picture of a man on a Bullet 350cc with the caption: 'Everything a man needs. And more.')

Due to the lack of small helmet sizes, children under three were exempt from this rule, and there was no mention of a maximum number of passengers. The most I saw on a scooter was five people: the rider, a passenger and three children. And this was on a steep mountain track.

I imagine there would be a lot of opposition if a limit were imposed on passenger numbers, as those scooters are our equivalent of the family car. And I was grateful there were so few private cars on the road: I had enough trouble with the trucks, the buses, the bullock carts, the scooters, the bicycles, the goats, the cows and the dogs.

I did feel sorry for the dogs; everyday I saw at least a couple dead. It's not really surprising, since they tend to use the road as a place to have a nap. Perhaps they look at the sacred cows and mistakenly conclude that vehicles will do anything to avoid hitting an animal...

~~~~~~~~~~~~

After my first day out of Dharamsala I stayed in Mandi – a small provincial town in the foothills of the Himalayas – in a hotel called the Raj Mahal, which means 'palace of the king'. Although not a palace, it contained the furniture and paintings of the ex-Maharaja of the region. The owner, who used to be a Maharaja himself, once had a real palace on a hill outside the town, which his son told me became a government office. Now the family lived in this beautiful, rambling townhouse, part of which had been converted into a hotel.

The rooms were filled with antiques from India and Tibet, and with colonial portraits showing the Maharajas in their full regalia of jewels, medals, luxurious jackets and extravagant turbans. Hung on a wall in one of the many corridors was an autographed photograph of Queen Victoria as a young woman.

Rajesh, the son of the ex-Maharaja, ran the hotel. He was 26 years old and had recently moved to Mandi. Previously he'd lived in Pune – a fast-moving and very modern town near Mumbai.

Rajesh invited me to join him for a drive in the mountains and dinner at the house of a friend of his. We drove up to Rewalsar Lake – a lake sacred to Hindus, Sikhs and Buddhists. Like in Amritsar, the water here was filled with holy fish, one of which had a large ring through its nose. Nobody could tell me why. During the drive to and from the lake, I sat nervously in the passenger seat while Rajesh took every hairpin with the screeches of a Formula One driver.

'It must be a nice change for you not to ride your bike,' Rajesh suggested. 'You don't have to worry about the road and you can enjoy the scenery.'

I could only manage a nod.

Just as the sun was coming down we reached the house of his friend Vikram and his mother Minal. Their home was built on top of a hill in large grounds, with a view of the snow-capped High Himalayas, which were now stained orange and purple. Each of the four bedrooms had an en-suite bathroom, and the servant quarters were down in the garden.

Vikram was a tall, very fair man in his mid-twenties who had recently become engaged through an arranged alliance to a young woman from Rajasthan. Like Rajesh, Vikram spoke perfect English, having been through English-language boarding schools in India. His mother, Minal, must have been in her mid-forties and was very beautiful. She had that ephemeral quality seldom seen in Western women. Or is it just called great bone structure and a tiny frame?

During dinner, Minal invited me to stay at their home whenever I wanted. Initially I assumed this was one of those polite invitations one was supposed to decline with a grateful smile, but when she insisted, I promised to stay with them on my way back from Manali – the last outpost before the beginning of the High Himalayas.

After dinner, Rajesh drove me back to the hotel in Mandi and the next day I rode to Naggar, which used to be the capital of the Kullu region. It was now a sleepy town which had the attraction, for me, of having had its castle converted to a grand old hotel where I could spend the night.

The 400-year-old ramshackle stone-and-wood construction was perched on the side of a mountain overlooking a deep green valley, with the River Beas running through the middle. It was popular with tourists as a stop for lunch, but not as a place to stay: my room was the only one occupied. I asked the manager why this was, and he suggested that maybe the tourists were afraid of the ghosts said to haunt the castle. I think it probably had more to do with the cockroaches in the bathroom and the unreliable electricity supply...

After enjoying a short walk in the neighbouring woods, I rode on to the town of Manali, famous for the beauty of its surrounding mountains and the abundance of its marijuana crop. The latter explained in large part why it attracted hundreds of Western travellers who stayed here for months – if not years: they enjoyed top-quality hash for a tiny fraction of the price they'd pay back home.

I wasn't tempted. My last experiment with hash, five years previously, had put me off it for life. At the time I

was working for a fund management company that had
sent me on a business trip to Amsterdam. One evening,
after my meetings and still wearing my business suit, I
decided to explore the city on my own, so I walked around
and then stopped in a bar for a drink.

There I met an Englishman and his friends; he bought
me a beer and offered me his joint. Not wanting to appear
straight-laced, I pulled on it and almost choked. Fire down
my throat. After only my second puff I felt queasy and
decided to go back to my hotel. The Englishman tried to
accompany me – I think he was hoping for an invitation –
but eventually abandoned me while I sat on a low wall by
the canal, waiting for my head to clear.

After he left, everything started swooning before my
eyes and I was afraid I'd fall into the canal. It seemed like
a good idea at the time to lie down on the pavement in
front of the wall. Just for a little while.

The rest is a bit hazy. Some people tried to help me up,
but my whole body seemed to be made out of jelly. Soon
after, a police van pulled up, out of which came two
officers who subjected me to the good cop/bad cop
routine. The bad cop was obviously having trouble
believing that all I'd had was a couple beers and two puffs
of a joint, while the other one made sympathetic noises.
Eventually the two of them half-carried me into the police
van and deposited me at the police station.

I remember standing, holding onto the metal bars of
the check-in window, while the good cop emptied my
handbag. I had no identification on me except for my
business cards and a few credit cards.

Once the check-in formalities had been completed – a
process that appeared to consist of confiscating my
handbag, my belt and finding out the name of my hotel – I
was shown to my cell. With relief, I passed out on the
floor on top of a very thin mattress. Soon after, I was
woken by a doctor asking me to open my eyes as he shone
a bright light into them. Confirming I didn't need medical
attention, he left and the police let me go back to sleep.

In the morning the bad cop seemed to have metamorphosed into a nice man, and he even called a taxi to take me back to my hotel, where the receptionist smiled knowingly and said, 'I hear you had an eventful night.'

I cringed in embarrassment. Obviously the police had called to check I was indeed staying there.

Smoking hash may be legal in Amsterdam, but not being able to handle it isn't.

In Manali, possession is illegal and carries a possible sentence of 10 years for a first offence. However, this doesn't stop people from smoking it in public – including in the post office, where I saw an employee behind the counter with a joint hanging off his lips.

There was a disproportionate number of Israeli tourists in Manali, despite Israel being such a small country. At a guess, I'd say half the foreign tourists were Israelis. And many spent their days in a trip of their own. Such was the scale of the problem that an Israeli government official had recently been to the area to see what could be done to discourage them. I fail to see what conclusions he might've reached: hash was cheap, abundant and easy to get ahold of. In fact you don't even have to *buy* it: you could just walk into a field and roll yourself a joint.

In addition, the local police were apparently not doing much to crackdown on it, since it brought in the tourists and provided a profitable cash crop – and, some people say, a sizeable kickback for the policemen.

When I came out of the post office in Manali I found my Australian friends, Greg and Jess, waiting for me by my bike. Again they'd recognised it from all its dents. They'd come up from Chamba on a slightly different route and arrived in Manali a few days before me. We decided to stay in the same guesthouse – an isolated place 10km away from the main town.

When I'd first arrived, the weather had been warm enough to walk around in a t-shirt, but overnight it dropped to minus five degrees and I woke up to find four inches of snow on the ground.

Since it was already snowing here at 2,000 metres, my plan to ride further up into the mountains was abandoned. As soon as the roads cleared up I'd turn around and head towards Rajasthan, where it's always warm.

Snowed in, Greg, Jess and I spent the day in their hotel room, sitting near the wood burning stove while reading, writing, playing cards and eating chocolates. It was fun for the first few hours, but then I developed the beginnings of a headache and a stomach ache. For a little while I imagined it was the long-awaited first bout of some sort of gut-wrenching, bowel-churning, fever-causing ogre bacteria: after more than a month in India I'd still not had that experience.

I knew in great detail what to expect, because many Western tourists liked to talk – usually at the dinner table – about how sick they'd been in India.

You'd be eating a not-particularly-appetising plate of stone-sprinkled rice with a brown sauce of lentils, when someone – usually a beautiful blond waif – would launch into the Intestinal Confessional.

'This is the first meal I've eaten for four days. I've been shut up in my room, puking my brains out. I don't know what did it. Maybe it was what I ate at that road-side dhaba. I'm going to get a stool test tomorrow to make sure it's not dysentery.' Then she'd add for good measure, 'That's if I can collect some stool. Right now it's more like a brown liquidy sauce coming out that end.'

I'd look down at my plate of lentils.

'At least I'll have great cheekbones when I go home!' she'd add, laughing.

I, however, have the intestines of a goat. After a month of travelling I'd only succumbed to a cold, which I'd dealt with by eating lots of sweets ('feed a cold' and all that…). It seemed almost obscene to be travelling in a country where many people don't have enough to eat and to complain that I hadn't lost any weight.

That said, even the little irritating bowel syndrome of a girl would've had difficulty looking gorgeous in my biking gear. None of that sexy leather look for me – more the Michelin Man look, with the addition of a thick coating of black diesel dirt on my face.

This was my riding gear in the mountains:

- Thermal long johns
- Thermal t-shirt
- Two pairs of socks
- Jeans
- Long-sleeved man's shirt
- Fleece cardigan
- Thick leather jacket with detachable fur lining
- Thick brown waterproofs bought in England (which turned out to be useless in anything more than a light drizzle)
- Leather hiking boots (I later wished I'd put heavy-duty masking tape around the top of the right foot to protect the leather from damage caused by changing the gears)
- Red hiking gaiters – useful for preventing the odd splash from filling my boots
- Leather motorcycle gloves bought in England, with an additional pair of thin lining gloves for the cold
- Neck scarf made out of a length of cotton bought in Kashmir; originally with a pattern of black-and-white squares that soon became a murky brownish/greyish tone
- Full-face white helmet bought in England for more money than most Indians earn in a year.

In the evening, in our guesthouse near Manali, Greg, Jess and I continued to huddle around the wood stove. We listened to the thunder and watched the falling snow and the lightning. Because of all the clouds – we were actually in the *middle* of a cloud – the lightning was a bright light with no obvious source that revealed nothing but more white cloud.

We sat there convinced we were probably dying of carbon monoxide poisoning but unwilling to open up the window to the cold. Even with enough food, plenty of wood to burn and good company, the time went by slowly. There are limits to how many card games you can play. And reading was out of the question, since the electricity in the whole valley had been out since the beginning of the snow storm.

According to the owner of the guesthouse, snow had come early that year. He was very concerned about it, because the hay was still spread out in the fields and cobs of corns were out to dry on the roof tops, for flour and animal winter feed.

The next morning we woke to grey skies, falling sleet, and slush everywhere. Should we stay another day and hope that tomorrow would be warmer still, or should we make our escape while we still could? My Australian friends decided to wait for better weather. I hesitated all morning, but by noon the sky seemed clearer and the sleet had become a light drizzle, so I went – or rather skidded – back down the valley.

After only half an hour the light drizzle turned into full-fledged rain. Riding a bike can be very difficult in these conditions; it took me five hours to cover the 90km back to Mandi. My waterproofs once again turned out to be completely ineffective, and eventually (albeit far too late) I took the plastic sheeting covering my luggage and tied it around my waist like a skirt. My leather jacket also became drenched. My boots, of course, were filled with water and my hands were numb with the cold.

I stopped at a roadside café for a very comforting cup of tea, and caused quite a sensation with the half-dozen truck drivers sheltering from the rain.

'You have come from Manali!' one of them exclaimed.

'You are very brave,' another one commented.

They invited me to join them for a hot drink.

First we had the usual questions: 'Where are you from?', 'What is your good name?', 'Are you married?', 'How much did you pay for your mo'bike?'

Then the men started talking amongst themselves and giggling. Yes – even truck drivers with big moustaches giggle.

One of them spoke good English and I asked him to translate.

'It is nothing. They are saying silly things.'

'What are they saying? It's about me, isn't it?'

He tried to fob me off. 'They are ignorant people. Not educated.'

I insisted and eventually he explained, 'They are asking if you are a man or a woman. They are being silly people.' He laughed with embarrassment. 'They are thinking you are a lady.'

After the truck drivers left, another patron came up to my table, grabbed his crotch and asked, 'You want?'

I still wonder if he thought he was propositioning a man or a woman.

Later, as arranged, I went to stay with my friends, Vikram and his mother Minal. They were preparing for a religious ceremony in their house – a 'puja' to give thanks for the birth of Minal's grandson.

In the morning the local priest set up for the ceremony on the terrace. He built a small campfire and decorated the ground around it with geometric shapes drawn with turmeric powder and flour. By the fire, he'd placed jars of oils and spices.

'What are the jars for?' I asked Vikram.

'When the priest is finished with all the preparations, we will sit around the flames, chant prayers and make offerings of spices and oils into the flames.'

'Does the priest charge for leading the puja?'

'He does not charge money but we will give clothes for him and his wife as well as some gold statuettes of the gods.'

Minal added, laughing, 'He's already given us the list of the clothes that he wants.' She pulled it out. 'He wants slippers for himself and his wife, three shirts, two shawls…'

I noticed the priest was wearing a gold Tissot watch: at least they should be grateful he wasn't asking for another one.

Neither Vikram nor his mother seemed particularly convinced by the ceremony. Vikram called it 'mumbo-jumbo' – though I wonder if that was because he thought it was what I expected him to say – and Minal told me she didn't really know if she believed in the ceremony but felt as the grandmother she had to do it; otherwise her daughter may feel hurt.

Although they showed scepticism about the ceremony, both Vikram and Minal believed in the priest's ability to tell people's fortunes, and they asked him to do this for me. The priest looked carefully at both my hands and my face for a while and said, via Vikram's translation, that I had recently undergone a major separation and left my job to come to India. But he thought this had been made a mistake. In addition, he could see that I'd been very hurt in the past and needed to learn to trust again. Now was a difficult time and I was under the nefarious influence of Saturn; to counteract this I'd need to buy myself a ring with a sapphire of two grams. I should put this ring under my pillow, and if I slept well and had good dreams I should wear the jewel on my right ring finger. He also said I'd need to pray very hard if I hoped ever to have a child. Finally, he gave me the business card of a good jeweller in town.

As I was preparing to leave my friends and resume my journey, Minal said, 'I'd love to come with you down to Rajasthan. That's where my family comes from.'

Minal was the widow of the son of a Himalayan Maharajah, and she herself was from a royal family in Rajasthan. When she visited Delhi she stayed with relatives who lived in the Presidential Palace. She also told me her father was a famous polo player and the one and only person in the world who'd scored a goal in two shots from one end of the field to the other. Supposedly that's even more outstanding than a hole-in-one in golf.

'You want to come? That's a great idea!' I exclaimed. 'I can take you on the back on my bike. That would be *so* much fun.'

She laughed nervously and turned to her son.

'But Mummy, you'd be terrified and probably cause Michèle to have an accident with all your screams of terror.'

Vikram looked by far the more terrified of the two.

It was a shame she didn't join me: Minal was a lovely person and I would've really enjoyed her company. She also clearly knew many influential people in India and could have shown me another side of the country.

Chapter 7
Soft porn in Shimla

Heading south, I stopped for a couple nights at a guesthouse in the small mountain village of Tatapani, famous for its hot springs. After a previous unpleasant night in a damp and cold room, a day of lazing around in the hot baths and reading a big fat bestseller helped ease my stiff joints.

On the second evening, while eating at the guesthouse, I met a Sikh man and his Irish girlfriend. We were the only guests in the dining room, and they invited me to share a bottle of beer they'd smuggled into the alcohol-free restaurant. The bottle was wrapped in brown paper and placed on the floor between servings. I doubt very much it fooled the waiter, who stood against the wall observing us.

Lalit, the Sikh man, was extremely good-looking, with an intelligent, alert and slightly amused expression. And since he didn't wear a turban, I could admire his thick, shiny, long black hair.

Both he and Mary, the Irish woman, worked as tour guides in India, though for different companies. They'd just come back from the Spiti Valley, high up in the Himalayas, and described it as an intensely beautiful mountain desert, with a lunar feel. Although it was three days north of Tatapani, and in the opposite direction to where I was eventually heading, they assured me it was well worth the detour and encouraged me to visit.

When we'd drained one large bottle of beer, Mary pulled out of her shoulder bag an equally badly camouflaged second bottle. Once that was finished we decided to transfer to the hot spring to end the evening with a long soak and a bottle of rum I had in my room.

We walked to the back of the hotel's garden and into a small hut built around the hot tub. The flimsy roof was made of pieces of corrugated iron, and through one of the gaps between the sheets of metal we could see the moon shimmering in a clear frosty sky.

Mary was lying in the steaming water with her head resting against the side of the tub. Looking up, she said, 'Last time I saw such a beautiful moon was when two boys killed themselves to save my life. I was in a small town near Delhi with a group of American tourists; we'd finished dinner and I decided to go for a walk alone on the outskirts of town. There was a small lake there. It was a lovely evening, the moon was out, and I could see water buffaloes silhouetted against the sky.

'Suddenly a scooter came speeding towards me without its headlight on. There were two people on it and I could see their faces really well. I remember the shock in their eyes when they realised they were going to hit me. At the last moment, the boy riding the scooter swerved to the left and into the barbed wire separating the road from the field.'

Mary paused to sip from her glass of rum. 'They both died as the wire cut through their throats. If they'd swerved to the right they would have gone into the water: I suppose they didn't see the wires.'

'And then what happened?' Lalit asked.

'People came out running. You know what it's like here: you think you're all alone but there's always people around. There was a lot of noise but I don't really remember much. Somebody brought me back to the hotel in an auto-rickshaw, and later that evening the police came to ask me what had happened.

'The next day I sent a message to the families of the boys asking if I could do something for them. They never answered.'

~~~~~~~~~~~

In the morning, with a tender head, I decided to follow Lalit and Mary's advice and head towards the Spiti Valley.

En route, during the first day I rode on near-empty roads carved out of the mountains. In many places I could see any incoming traffic, so I had great fun leaning into the bends and generally trying to ride smoothly and sinuously. I reached the town of Rampur quite late, and had difficulty finding a hotel with a vacancy as the town was holding its annual trade fair. Eventually a hotel owner called around and located me an overpriced and damp room.

The next day I left at six in the morning to continue on my way. After four hours on a progressively deteriorating road I passed a roadwork site; as I slowly manoeuvred the bike around bulldozers and three-feet-high mounds of gravel, a young man ran up behind me and grabbed the back of my bike. I ignored him, thinking he just wanted to hitch a lift. (In the past I'd had teenagers try to hitch a ride that way.) I even accelerated in an attempt to make him lose his grip.

But he held on and shouted, 'Stop! Dynamite!'

Dynamite? That stopped me.

He led me to the side of the road, where I joined a group of workers standing against the wall of the mountain awaiting the explosion.

BANG!

Again we waited.

BANG!

After the second explosion they returned to work and assured me there would be no more for a while.

I continued my journey and the road continued to deteriorate, until it became a dry river-bed – and then a wet river-bed. I pulled over and waded in to measure the depth of the water: just below the knee. But the large rocks under the water could be a problem. Should I go on?

While I debated with myself, I heard the sound of stones falling down the mountain. I looked up and saw a soldier running down the steep slope, onto the road and towards me. He looked in a hurry to speak to me.

'No go through! Bad road. Much rocks and water.'

He emphasised his point by making large sweeping

movements with the rifle on his shoulder.

In no mood to argue with a man carrying a gun, I turned back towards Rampur, almost relieved that the decision had been made for me. The road was obviously going to be very difficult, and there was always the risk of getting stuck due to early snow. In addition, my leaking fork seals meant that I had almost no suspension in the front, and every bump in the road could be felt throughout my whole body.

The bike's second 3,000-kilometre service was now due and I needed to find an Enfield garage. Furthermore, other things on the bike needed attention: the gears kept getting stuck, the brake light was always on and the indicators had stopped working.

Still, it would have been nice to go to Spiti; at one point I would have been in sight of Tibet. But like Ladakh, that would have to wait for next summer when the roads were better. The upside was that I could now spend some time visiting the annual fair in Rampur.

~~~~~~~~~~

This could be a long night, I thought to myself as I sat in the hotel's restaurant.

Again I'd had trouble finding a room in Rampur. After visiting every hotel in town, the owner of this hotel kindly offered his dining-room, which would only become available as my bedroom after midnight.

I tried to stay out as late as possible but ran out of activities after I'd gone around the annual fair twice, taken a ride on the rickety Ferris wheel, sampled freshly squeezed orange juice with salt (very refreshing), bought myself a beige woollen shawl, and had my picture taken at a photographer's stall through the window of a mock cardboard minibus. There I'd agreed to a request from a young boy to pose with him: instantly a crowd materialised and four other men asked for the same.

I walked around the market stalls and watched the

shepherds, with their Asiatic features, selling their hand-woven woollen clothing and blankets and buying ready-made clothes, kitchen utensils and other manufactured goods.

By seven in the evening the cold night forced me back to my hotel, and I slowly watched the evening go by while trying to ignore the TV screen where a flickering video tape of a marriage was playing at very high volume. I remembered with apprehension being told that Indian weddings went on for days. I tried reading but the noise intruded. So instead I watched the other people in the restaurant busily making deals, arranging marriages (according to one of the waiters) and catching up on each other's news.

I was also stressing about blankets: in my obsession with travelling light, I'd decided not to carry a sleeping bag. I asked the hotel owner if he had any blankets and he said yes, but I wasn't convinced he really understood the question.

I shouldn't have worried. Not only did the owner supply me with a warm duvet, but he also came up with a bed frame and a mattress. I shared the dining room with him and a couple of his waiters. Nobody snored and I had a great night's sleep – although I did wake myself up at four in the morning, laughing. I probably woke the others up too, but they were too polite to mention it.

The next day, Big Thumper refused to start: the decompressor needle wouldn't budge from the zero mark. I got my bike manual out to see if I could sort it out myself, but the crucial pages had been ripped out of the book. Of course, I hadn't thought to check that the manual was intact when I bought the bike.

The hotel manager called the town's motorcycle mechanic, who arrived half an hour later. He immediately identified a loose cable behind the battery, stuck it into the relevant socket and the bike started. Simple when you know how. The call-out charge and the repair cost me $1.50. (He only wanted a dollar but I was feeling extravagant.)

I then rode for five hours to Shimla – a major hill station built by the British during the Raj. As the heat in April/May became too intense for the foreigners in Delhi, many British officials, and almost all the wives, moved up to Shimla. It was renowned for its lavish parties and – with husbands often absent – illicit affairs.

It's quite a sizeable town, built on very steep hills. During British reign, the main shopping road – The Mall – was forbidden to both dogs and Indians. Today, Shimla is a popular destination for well-to-do Indian tourists, often dressed in Western clothes.

For the first time since I'd left Delhi a month previously, I saw women in jeans and with short hair, rather than long-haired and in punjabis. I also saw many honeymooners. Some were looking very uncomfortable with each other, while others bubbled with happiness, making the others appear even more awkward.

Thinking it'd be fun to go to the cinema, I bought a ticket to see an English-language film called *Love Beach*. There were only a few dozen people in the audience, so I was perplexed when a man took the seat right next to me. Still, he seemed inoffensive, and as we waited for the film to begin he introduced himself as an engineer from Delhi, here on his holidays. The lights dimmed and the title credits rolled on.

The background to the credits was a scene at the beach – a *nude* scene at the beach. It prompted numerous wolf whistles from the audience.

Shit.

I cleared my voice. 'Is this a sex film?' I asked my neighbour.

He hesitated. 'Well, sort of. Why? Are you embarrassed?'

You bet.

Actually, it could've been fun to see the film and the audience's reaction to it. But what I found embarrassing was imagining what my neighbour and others in the audience would think of me if I sat through it. With as much dignity as possible (i.e. none), I walked out.

Perhaps the film's title should have given me a clue; if not that, then the exclusively male audience should've done the trick. But I'd thought India was a conservative country, and that porn films wouldn't be shown in mainstream cinemas – especially one next door to a YMCA. I was forgetting that India is the home of the Kama Sutra.

Maybe as a reaction to the film, my next overnight stop was in the Working Women's Hostel in the town of Chandigarh – a hostel catering to college students and unmarried office workers.

I decided to stay here for a couple of days while the local dealer serviced my bike.

Meals were served in the dining room and I ate with the young women. At breakfast one morning I shared my table with a Kashmiri student; we introduced ourselves and I told her she came from a very beautiful state.

She smiled proudly. 'Oh, you have visited Kashmir. When was that?'

'Just a month ago.'

'You mean this year?' she asked, incredulously.

'Well, yes,' I admitted, a bit shamefaced.

She gasped. 'You shouldn't go there! It's very dangerous for tourists. People have been kidnapped and killed.'

There was nothing I could say.

She got up from the breakfast table and walked away, shaking her head and repeating, 'You shouldn't go there.'

If I'd had any doubts about whether going to Kashmir had been a sensible idea, I didn't now. True, I'd asked people's advice before going, but they were tourists who'd just returned from there. *Of course* they wouldn't say it was too dangerous, since they'd had no trouble. I'd also asked people in Kashmir itself, but their livelihood generally depended on tourists. They too wouldn't say if it were dangerous – though my houseboat owner had told me some parts of Srinagar were definitely out of bounds. Naturally, I'm glad I went, as I encountered no incidents and had the opportunity to meet an interesting people and see wonderful scenery. However, since then I've read so many reports of bombings and shootings that I think I was probably just lucky not to experience any difficulties.

That evening I befriended the two young women staying in the room next to mine and they invited me for a chat in their room after dinner. Kaajal and Uma were both students in the local business college. Kaajal, who was very pretty, had a boyfriend who worked as an engineer. They were planning to get married as soon as she finished her studies – although Kaajal would have preferred to get married right away.

'But what about your degree?' I asked.

She replied, 'I don't care about that. I'm so happy with him, I want to get married right now. But he says I should finish my studies first so that I can have a good job before we have children.'

A sensible man, I thought.

The other woman, Uma, also planned to get married soon after graduation, but she hadn't yet found her future husband. Her parents were now looking on her behalf.

She'd sent them a portrait she'd recently had taken in a professional photographic studio to show to interested grooms. I asked to see it. It looked nothing like her: Uma was a very dark woman with rather coarse features, but on the picture her skin appeared very fair, with subtle lighting softening her features and what could not be softened camouflaged under thick make-up. She looked like a glamorous film star.

I asked her, 'What kind of man do you hope to marry?'

'I don't know,' she sighed, with a dreamy look in her eyes. 'My parents will choose.'

'And you trust their choice?' I asked.

'Yes, it is our tradition in India. It's not usual for people to choose like Kaajal. Her parents are very modern.'

'What kind of man do you hope they will choose for you?'

'A gentle man who's nice looking and has a good position. And,' Uma added, laughing, 'who has a nice mother!'

~~~~~~~~~~

While in Chandigarh, I found an office with internet access and received an e-mail from a friend in London asking how I coped with all the poverty and the beggars in India.

Beggars. Poverty. Indians usually get offended when foreigners focus on these things.

'Can't you write about something else?' they ask.

'I've been to New York/London/Paris, they have many beggars there too!' they point out.

True. But there are more of them here, and they're a lot more persistent.

My concession to these nationalistic sensibilities was to wait until now before bringing up the subject.

How did I 'cope' with them? At first I was shocked by their number and physical condition, but after a while I became more accustomed. Once I was able to look beyond the rotten extremities of the lepers, beyond the tumours the size of tennis balls on men's necks, beyond the fly-invested sores on children's feet... and had the courage to look at their faces – at their eyes – so that I could see them as individuals rather than just grossly mutilated bodies, then they became less scary. I made a rule that I would give them 100 rupees a day.

However, as the months went on I began to resent the beggars' assumption that I was an easy touch, and I made another rule: I'd only give to those too old or too ill to work – never to children or people who used children. It wasn't that I thought the kids less needy than their parents; but I feared they were being run by criminal gangs who took all their earnings.

It could get awkward. For instance, while I was waiting for my bike to be serviced in Chandigarh, an old lady in a torn sari with a child of about five asked me for money. I said no, but she insisted. She pointed to the little girl, pushing her towards me and bringing her fingers to her mouth in a gesture of hunger. I kept on saying no but she continued for a few long minutes. People were looking at us and I felt embarrassed. Were they thinking here was another rich tourist who could afford an Enfield 500 but wouldn't give even a few rupees? Did I really have the right to decide who was worthy of my spare change? It made no difference to me but all the difference to them. Eventually I succumbed and gave the old lady 50 rupees.

Towards the end of my trip, however, after almost a year in India, I became even more hardened. Some days it seemed I could blind myself to anything I found unpleasant. I'd stop seeing the disfigured beggars, or the precarious slum dwellings alongside the railway tracks, or the deformed, bloated and limping cows walking aimlessly through traffic jams, or the dirty naked children playing in rubbish dumps while their parents painstakingly looked for reusable items.

I learned to look at a beautiful sunset while keeping my gaze higher than the pile of empty bottles and soiled paper at my feet, or the dirty, snotty-nosed beggar child pulling at my shirtsleeve while murmuring in a plaintive voice. My compassion was replaced at best by a blindness and deafness, and at worst by irritation – whether directed at them, or myself, I'm not sure.

Sometimes I'd give a few rupees just to make the beggar disappear. Other times I'd get angry with their constant whining, mutter some nasty remark in English and walk away.

Only occasionally did I give with a smile. At the end of my trip, in a short-lived fit of guilt, I had a week of giving 50 rupee notes to almost every beggar I saw.

Chapter 8
Down in Rajasthan

To avoid going through Delhi again on my way from the Himalayas to Rajasthan, I decided to cross the state of Punjab instead. The cold of the mountains was quickly replaced with the heat of the plains, and after a long day on the bike it was great to arrive in Bathinda, order a cold beer on room service and watch *BBC World* in the city's top hotel.

A bit later, the owner of the hotel – a tall man dressed in beige trousers, a white shirt and a shocking pink turban – invited me for a cold drink and a chat in his office. Because, once again, I'd lied and put journalist as my profession in the hotel register, he wished to speak to me about the state of the tourism industry in Punjab.

'You must write about our beautiful Punjab, madam. People are afraid to come here because they remember the violence of before.'

He explained that for many years the state of Punjab had suffered from a very violent independence movement that had kept tourists away. The visitors were yet to return, and this man's business was suffering.

He got up from his desk to search for some papers in his cabinet. 'Look. Also me, I am a journalist. Here are some articles I have been writing about tourist development in Punjab.'

He asked me to read his articles. The following is a direct quote:

'Its known fact that Punjab had passed through a decade under the dark sheet of Terrorism. The fear of Terrorism had set so deep in the minds of all citizens in India & Abroad that once who use to claim proudly, that they belong to Punjab were scared even to visit Punjab.

'We got back, the light, the coloures & the life in

Punjab after the years of struggle and scarifies made by thousands of youths, Politicians, & the citizens of India. During this course, the land so called full of history & livelore was totally cut off from Tourism activities.'

The hotel owner kept me in his office for over two hours to make sure he'd convinced me that Punjab was a great destination for tourists, and that I should tell the world. I promised him I'd write about it…

In truth, I don't think there is much to attract the tourist to Punjab. There's the Golden Temple in Amritsar, which is beautiful, and a fort in Bathinda, which is attractive in a rambling, dilapidated sort of way. But little apart from that. And the scenery, after the Himalayas, is disappointing: flat agricultural land with rivers so polluted it looks like someone's running a giant malodorous bubble bath. However, I can say that the Punjabi people seem to be very friendly and relatively affluent. And the men are very good-looking.

~~~~~~~~~~

Good grief! I decided not to answer the door anymore; within two hours of checking into my hotel in Ganganagar I'd had *eight* visits from the staff.

Visit number one: 'Excuse me madam, checking the hot water working,' the manager announced as he walked into my room, without knocking, and straight into the bathroom.

Visit number two came five minutes later: 'Checking the A/C working, madam.'

Ten minutes later, visit number three: I heard a knock but I was on the toilet and before I had time to get my clothing back on the manager had entered my bedroom.

'Madam?'

'Don't come in!' I shouted as I lunged to close the bathroom door.

'Madam. I have article for you to read.'

'Leave it there on my bed and please leave my room.'

He ignored me and said, 'I am waiting to show you.'

'I don't want you to wait for me,' I grumbled under my breath as I pulled my trousers back up and entered the bedroom.

'Look, madam. I find an article about the fort in Ganganagar. It is in Hindi but I can translate for you. It says that...'

I interrupted him, 'Thank you, I have information in my book about the fort [I didn't]. Is it alright if I take a bath now?'

Twenty minutes later I had visit number four, but this time I'd put a chair against the door to lock it so he had to wait until I'd dried and dressed myself.

I opened the door.

'Room service?' the manager asked.

'I'll call you when I want to order food,' I laughed as I virtually closed the door on him.

Ten minutes later he was back for visit number five: 'Bringing you soap and towel.'

A bit late, I thought. I've already washed.

Half an hour later, another knock. Visit number six. I decided not to answer this time.

'Open. Police!' a gruff voice ordered.

I opened to find the manager standing alongside a man in uniform.

'Your passport, madam,' the policeman demanded. 'What are you doing here? You are going to Pakistan?'

We were 30km from the border.

'No, I'm just on my way to Rajasthan,' I replied.

'Well, you must not try to go to Pakistan. It is illegal to cross here. You will be shot.' As he handed me back my passport, he added with a little bow and a smile, 'I am wishing you a pleasant journey.'

After another half hour the manager came back with his younger brother. Visit number seven.

'My brother wants to meet with you.'

'Nice to meet you,' I lied as I shook his brother's limp hand.

The brother did little except giggle and gawk.

'Bye, then,' I said as I slowly closed my door.

Ten minutes later I got my eighth and final visit from the manager.

'You have goods from Britain to sell, madam?'

'What do you mean?' I asked, exasperated.

'Things from Britain. I like things from outside India.'

With a sigh, I let him in as I rummaged through my luggage and pulled out a collection of postcards showing famous sights of London. 'These are pictures of my home city. Would you like one?'

After a quick glance through them, he handed them back and replied. 'No, thank you. You not have picture of Queen Diana?'

To top it all off, the next morning, when it came to paying my bill, the manager wouldn't give me my change until I'd met his daughter. I had to wait for her to come from their home so that she could practice her English with me while her father beamed. She was in fact very nice, and slightly embarrassed by the situation.

Finally on the road, I entered the western desert of Rajasthan, which would eventually turn into sand dunes but at this stage was more rocks and shrubs.

After a few hours of riding I wanted to stop and stretch my legs. Usually I'd just stop for a few minutes, because it only took that long before a scooter rider or a cyclist would pull over for a chat or just a stare. But this time I wanted a quiet, uninterrupted break to enjoy the silence of the desert, so I turned off on a dirt track, pushed Big Thumper behind some shrubs and stretched out in the sun with my biscuits and water bottle.

Half an hour later, feeling well rested, I got back on the bike, only to discover it was stuck in the sand. I heaved, revved and pushed, but my bike just sank further. So much for my desire to be left alone. Where were all those curious but helpful people now?

Eventually I managed to get the bike out on my own by unloading it and putting some rocks and branches under the wheels.

~~~~~~~~~~~

Jainism is a minority religion in India that began in 500BC as a reformist movement against the dominance of the priest caste in Hinduism. Jains believe very strongly in reincarnation and they stress the importance of not killing any living thing. In the courtyard of the beautiful three-storied Bhandasar Jain temple at Bikaner – a large town in the middle of the Thar desert in Rajasthan – I saw a woman carrying a feathered broom and sweeping the ground in front of her feet as she walked so that she wouldn't accidentally kill some poor ant. And the man who showed me around the temple wore a cloth mask over his mouth so as not to swallow any insects.

After visiting the Jain temple I went to a Hindu temple 30km outside Bikaner, where Hindus revere small rats as future incarnations. There must have been hundreds – if not thousands – of rats scrambling on the polished stone floor of this small temple. The Hindus believe each one will be reincarnated into a saddhu. Since in all temples you have to take off your shoes, I walked around barefoot, and as I crouched to take a photo of some of the rats I felt something tickling the top of my foot: it was one of the rodents sniffing around my feet.

An elderly man standing nearby chuckled. 'You are lucky. The rat is giving you good luck.'

'Really?' I said, doubtfully, trying not to flinch.

'Yes, you are lucky because you come here. This is a very good place, full of magic.' He looked down at my feet. 'This rat has chosen you and will help you in your next life. He will be your teacher, your guru.'

~~~~~~~~~~~

The next morning, back in Bikaner, as I came down the stairway in my hotel I noticed two men at the reception watching me. The taller was asking the other one a question in Hindi, and although I couldn't understand what he was saying, I recognised the words 'lady' and 'gent' in English.

Before his friend could respond, I answered, 'I'm a lady.'

Embarrassed, they laughed and asked me if I spoke Hindi.

I replied, 'Only a few sentences, but I'm used to people thinking I'm a man, so when I heard "lady" and "gent" I knew what you were talking about.'

I loaded my bike and rode on to the small town of Pokaran to visit its fourteenth-century citadel. There were very few places to stay, but luckily I found a room in a grand old hotel situated on the actual grounds of the fortress. I was the only guest. After checking in I wandered around the fort at sunset and was approached by a young man. Cue the usual questions.

'Hello madam, you are from?'

I answered. 'From England.'

He continued, 'What is your good name?' and, 'You are liking our India?'

I answered his questions and tried to move away.

He followed me. 'You have seen inside the fort? It has many rooms I can show you.'

Wearily, I said, 'Thank you, but I'm quite happy to wander around alone absorbing the atmosphere. I don't want a guide.'

He looked at me in surprise. 'But I'm not a guide, madam. I'm the manager of your hotel.'

I felt very embarrassed. It wasn't the first time I'd confused genuinely friendly people with the hustlers (those who con the tourists into a tour they don't want or into a shop where they get a 25% commission). If I'm not careful, I thought to myself, I could easily turn into one of those sour-faced tourists who reject all approaches and assume everybody is out to rip them off.

That night I got my first and long-anticipated stomach

bug. As I wallowed in my bed, drenched in sweat and self-pity, I wrote in my diary:

Was I mentioning a couple weeks ago my cast-iron stomach? Well, no longer. I'm never again commenting about my weight if the cure is a night like last night. In fact I won't have to, because I'm never, ever, eating again. It's a good thing I'm staying in such a nice hotel, with a private bathroom and a Western toilet. I saw plenty of it last night.

I wish I had someone here with me to listen to my moans instead of just this diary.

My stomach's cramping up. I feel nauseated. There's a man with a Black & Decker inside my skull drilling his way out of my eye sockets. Is that a jet plane revving up in my guts? Oh, no! It's taking off! Quick – to the toilet.

I'm back. Too sick to write.

Still feeling pretty shaky, I decided to go on to Jaisalmer, 100km away, where I could rest for a few days. This hotel in Pokaran, whilst lovely, was outside my usual budget and I knew Jaisalmer, famed for its fort and temples, would have many guesthouses and amenities geared to the Western traveller – including plain food and lots of English-speaking pharmacists.

Usually, if the roads were in reasonable condition – which they are in Rajasthan – I had no problem covering 200–300km in a day; that day, however, those 100km felt like a thousand. Fortunately the road was straight and near-empty, so my dizziness-induced wobbles didn't leave me splattered on the road. Still, perhaps I should have rested longer before getting back on my bike…

I diagnosed myself as having giardia. Not a difficult diagnosis, since giardia's most distinctive symptoms are burping and breaking wind, both of which smell like rotten eggs. At the chemist in Jaisalmer I bought some tinidazole, and a day later felt fine again. (You can buy all sorts of drugs here without a prescription.)

Still, I decided it'd be best to go back to bottled water – or at least filtered water. I'd been taking this 'living like the locals' thing a bit too far. In fact I'd gone from one extreme to another: when I'd first arrived in India the water had frightened me so much that I'd made sure I only breathed through my nose in the shower. However, as I'd stayed healthy I became more and more confident, and eventually decided if the Indians could drink it, so could I. Of course, as I later found out, most Indians − if they have access to it − only drink filtered water.

Jaisalmer, where I was now staying, is known as the 'Golden City' − a name well deserved due to the richly sculptured yellow sandstone buildings. The carved buildings are so intricate it's hard to believe they're not made out of wood. The town is dominated by a fortress and surrounded by the sand dunes of the desert. Although the city is very small, I quickly got lost in its labyrinth of narrow stone-paved alleyways.

As I was wandering around, I passed a window with an old lady drawing henna designs on a young woman's hands. I stopped to look and when she finished she did mine. She told me the markings would remain for a couple weeks.

My plan was to take off my bike gloves and show my hands to the next person who called me sir. If that failed, I also knew how to say 'I am a woman' in Hindi: 'mai ord hu' − although my pronunciation was so bad I sometimes felt I was just adding to the confusion.

~~~~~~~~~~~

I had a long day ahead of me: 300km from Jaisalmer to Jodhpur via a road that went through two animal reserves, a few villages and a lot of desert.

At two o'clock, having covered only 150km, I suddenly felt that tell-tale wobble in my steering: my second puncture.

The road was very narrow and there was no hard shoulder − just the sandy desert. With a lot of grunting and panting, I hauled the bike onto the roadside and left it positioned rather precariously on the soft sand with all my luggage, and walked back to the previous village – which was fortunately only 1km away.

What luck! This place had not just one puncture repair shop but two. (The many thorn bushes growing by the side of the road may have had something to do with it.)

I chose one of the shops and explained to the puncture wallah the problem, hoping he, or another man in the shop, would walk back with me to get the wheel. Instead he sent five very young boys – all younger than ten years old – to help me. We reached the bike and the children started pushing it out of the sand and onto the road: clearly they planned to push it all the way to the village.

I wasn't having any of that, so I got my tool bag and my manual out and set about getting the front wheel off. It took me quite some time as the bike wasn't very stable in the sand and the boys were constantly interrupting, trying to help, climbing onto the bike, looking through my bags, touching my jewellery, pointing at my hennaed hands... They were cute but not very helpful.

It'd nice to be able to say I took it all in good grace and with a smile. But no, I lost my temper.

I shouted, 'Don't touch that!' and, 'Give me back the spanner!'

I muttered, 'Don't you have a school to go to?'

They, of course, couldn't understand anything and found it very funny; they kept repeating my words and bursting into fits of giggles.

After an hour of swearing and sweating, I got the wheel off and led a procession of children back to the puncture wallah, who identified a damaged valve on the inner tube in addition to a big thorn in the tyre. It's just as well *anything* can be repaired in India, since, stupidly, I wasn't carrying a spare inner tube – and neither did he have one.

While the puncture wallah worked, I sat in the shade of the repair shop, sipping a soft drink and trying to get my calm back. Everything would get sorted out and I'd get to

Jodhpur before 10pm. So what if I had to ride at night? Since when was I scared of the dark?

Unfortunately, because I'd neglected to negotiate a price for the repair work before it had started, the puncture wallah tried to charge four times the going price. Under the amused gaze of the children, I argued with him for 10 minutes until he agreed to take only twice the going rate. With the wheel, I walked back to the bike accompanied by a group of now eight boys.

It took me another hour to get the wheel back on, during which time I became increasingly flustered. I kept dropping nuts and washers in the sand; it was obvious I didn't know what I was doing, and the children loved it. Each one had a suggestion – which they communicated with a great deal of gesturing and laughter – and each one wanted to handle the tools.

Eventually, we did get the wheel back on – minus the front brake – and I rode off, leaving them my biscuits.

I then covered 150km – most of them in the dark. If I hadn't been so stressed I might've enjoyed it. I saw a beautiful sunset, grouse, peacocks, antelopes and, of course, cattle, donkeys and camels. Just as the sun came down an antelope raced me alongside the road. It stayed with me for a little while until I gave up. (I claim the lack of front brake as my excuse for losing the race...)

Night fell very quickly, and because there was no moon I saw a myriad of stars.

Every quarter of an hour or so, a truck would come from the opposite direction. I don't know if it was my frame of mind (i.e. scared), but it certainly felt like they were heading straight for me. After a few close shaves, I pulled over off the road whenever a truck came. I was very tired but relieved when I eventually reached Jodhpur.

~~~~~~~~~~~~

My first day in Jodhpur was spent at the Enfield mechanic's getting my front brake reconnected and my clutch plates replaced, as it seemed I'd been riding the clutch.

The next day I went exploring. The city's dominated by yet another fort. Rajasthan is a state of warrior clans, the Rajputs, who seem to have spent most of recent history fighting – both each other and outside invaders; there's a fort in every town, and sometimes in villages too. But this fort is most impressive: it's located right in the centre of the city, on the top of a 100 metre-high cliff that rises up from the urban sprawl. It looks impregnable. The interior is both functional from a defence point of view and also opulent.

However, what I found most moving were the fifteen handprints of the Maharaja's fifteen wives that are displayed on the left of the main gate. These are known as Sati marks. They were left by the wives prior to burning themselves alive on his funeral pyre in the mid-nineteenth century. Thankfully this is no longer allowed, although I read there was a case in the late 1980s of a nineteen-year-old bride of only three months who burned herself on her husband's funeral pyre, holding his hand in her lap.

In the evening I treated myself to dinner in the banqueting hall of the Umaid Palace – now a luxury hotel – that was built by the Maharaja in the 1930s. It's an enormous building, not in my view in the best of taste, but it certainly has a majestic quality. It's made of marble and red sandstone, has massive pillars, stuffed leopards, antelopes and even a bear, very high ceilings and an enormous dome. The place is a few kilometres out of town, so I rode out on my motorbike, sneaked into the cloakroom in my bike gear, and emerged in my punjabi hoping I looked like I belonged there. The meal was wonderful, and there was even a live sitar and tabla concert. My only regret was that I ate too much southern fried chicken to sample the lemon soufflé. A welcome change from the usual rice and lentils...

I decided to break up the next part of my journey, from Jodhpur to Udaipur, by visiting Kumbhalgarh Fort, which was built in the fifteenth century. It stands on top of a big hill inside an imposing wall that stretches for over 10km around it. It was attacked many times in the past but only taken once. I did see a few other Western tourists there, but they were most definitely not of the backpacking variety – more of the 'hire your own car and driver' variety.

After visiting the fort I walked back to my bike, passing a group of Italian tourists and anticipating with pleasure the scene that I knew would inevitably follow. I pulled out the keys from my pouch and unlocked the chain from my bike. I could feel their eyes on me. With a little smile I turned to the Italian group and said, 'Hello! It's a lovely fort, isn't it?'

'Si, very nice,' a slightly overweight man with a baseball cap answered.

'This is yours?' he asked, pointing to Big Thumper.

'Oh, that? Yes, it's mine,' I replied with false modesty.

'You are riding it in India? On these roads? With these crazy drivers? Mama mia! Molto brava!'

'Oh, it's very kind of you to say that. But,' I added with a little shrug, 'it's really not that difficult.'

I put my helmet on and kick-started the bike under the admiring gaze of ten Italians, and with a little wave, I was off. It's childish, it's conceited, but it's *so* much fun.

I then rode to a major Hindu temple in the village of Nathdwara, 50km east. This temple is dedicated to Lord Krishna, who was one of the ten incarnations of Lord Vishnu, known as the Preserver, who was himself one of the three representations of an all-powerful God. I find it all very confusing. Anyway, the thing most people remember (well, me at least) about Lord Krishna was that he was the one who cavorted with all the beautiful shepherdesses.

Outside I met a woman who visited the temple with her family every year on a pilgrimage from Calcutta, 1,500km away. She told me that Lord Krishna was a favourite of the poorer Indians because he himself was raised by a poor peasant family, and that the temple had closed at lunchtime and would re-open at three thirty (when Lord Krishna is said to wake from his afternoon nap).

I stood with the woman outside the gates, alongside a few hundred other people. Then the gates opened and the crowd ran into the temple and into the room where Lord Krishna's statue stood. Everybody was laughing and chanting. My companion took my hand and I ran alongside her.

At the entrance to the room, the women separated from the men to go through a different door. As I went in, a guard stopped me.

'No, go back. Men other door.'

My lady companion vouched for my gender and I went in.

The large crowd was happy, and many threw coins at the statue. Next to me was a large woman dressed in a canary-yellow sari and wearing shiny bangles all the way up to her elbows. There was something a bit strange about her, and when she laughed I realised she was in fact a man. I'm sure of it: I even saw stubble on her chin. So the guard had tried to stop me but let a transvestite in?

Maybe, for the sake of symmetry, I should have stood in the men's section.

~~~~~~~~~~

After two months of travelling and being on my own most of the time, I was going through a down period, missing friends and family. I shut myself up in the beautiful town of Udaipur, 50km south, paying little attention to the lovely lake setting, the hills around it and the exotic palaces, and instead sat on the balcony outside my room, reading books about India and following the recent political developments on the radio and in newspapers.

After nearly four weeks of 'won't it/will it fall?' the

Indian parliament was dissolved when the Congress Party withdrew its support for the ruling Coalition. The Congress Party members didn't have to do this, but obviously they wanted to have another election because they thought they could win a majority. The President of India called for mid-term elections for around the end of February 1998.

In my discussions with Indians here, it seemed clear there was very little enthusiasm for another election – the last one having been less than two years ago. People were worried about sectarian violence and the cost of the ballot. Not surprising, considering the electorate consists of 630 million voters and there are more than 100 parties.

A shopkeeper in the town complained to me that the prices of staple goods such as sugar and rice always rose after an election: he spoke of a 10% to 20% hike. His biggest fear, however, was that the end result of all this could be that the BJP, the Hindu nationalist party, would come out as the winner and head the next government.

~~~~~~~~~~~~

'Is it a he or a she?' one of the young girls asked in a loud whisper to her two friends.

I looked up at them, and before her friends could answer I said in a clear voice, 'It's a she.'

The three girls looked down in embarrassment and the first one mumbled, 'Oh, sorry, sorry,' before running away towards the exit of the Dilwara Jain temples in Mount Abu.

Being taken for a man was becoming routine; I should've been used to it by now. At first I'd found it amusing, but right now it was upsetting me. I've never liked labels, whether they be of nationality, race, class, religion or profession. They're used to categorise people into neat little boxes. You become known as the label on the box, and everyone you meet has a preconception of what that label represents. However, it seems there's one label I do identify with: that of woman. I'm not sure what it means in practice, but I do want people to treat me as female and not as a rather effeminate man.

It was unsettling to have something that seemed so intrinsic to my identity put into question. I wondered whether this was a similar – but much less intense – feeling to what transsexuals experience: to be treated as men when they feel they're women, or vice versa.

I considered wearing bigger earrings, since many Indian men wear small earrings (one in each ear) like the kind I wore; but they would dig into my neck when I wore the helmet. I thought about wearing more feminine clothes or shoes, but again that wouldn't be possible on the motorcycle. And I wasn't willing to grow my hair. So I supposed I'd just have to grin and bear it.

Many months later I became so accustomed to being taken for a man that it did eventually stop bothering me so much. In any case, there was something rather amusing about fooling people. One thing I did notice is that when people saw me as a man they paid much less attention to me than when they saw me as a woman. By that I don't just mean sexual attention, but also that I generated more curiosity as a woman. I suspect it was the rarity factor.

In these relatively early days, however, I was upset by the confusion, and I wandered around the Dilwara temples feeling rather ugly and paying little attention to my surroundings. After a little while I noticed an eerie silence and found myself alone in the most amazing building. Neither pictures nor words could possibly do it justice. I was surrounded, on all sides and above me, by white marble sculptures of people, elephants, chariots and flowers, so delicate and intricate it was almost impossible to comprehend how a hammer and chisel could have carved them out of blocks of rock.

This cheered me up.

Outside the temple, while I was unlocking my bike, an old man came up to me.

'Hello, and what is your good name?' he asked.

I answered and shook his hand.

'Forgive me for saying, but I'm glad you are smiling now.'

I laughed. 'What do you mean?'

'I saw you in the temple and you looked so sad, I felt bad. I thought you've come to my country and it's made you unhappy. But now I see you're not sad.'

I answered with something about being lost in my thoughts until I'd noticed how beautiful the temple was.

'I am glad.' The old man shook my hand again and said goodbye.

This wasn't the first time I'd been told how clearly my face reveals my emotions. I could never carry off a bluff.

You couldn't, however, say that the Indians I encountered had the same problem: it was impossible for me to tell what someone was thinking from his facial expression. Sometimes I'd be sitting on my bike in a small village, surrounded by fifty people, all staring impassively at me with what I can only call indifferent curiosity.

Have you ever turned around in a cinema theatre and looked at the audience? If so, you'll have seen an engrossed but blank look on the faces. Well, I felt like the cinema screen – and it was unnerving. People would give me eye contact but it was empty. Sometimes, if I tried to stare them out, they'd eventually look away, but I'd still feel like I'd lost because they'd given nothing away. This feels like a nation of poker players.

Chapter 9
Going through Gujarat

Big Thumper was beginning to give me trouble again: it was stalling, backfiring, and had little pick-up. The first mechanic in Udaipur diagnosed a dirty carburettor, but cleaning it didn't resolve the problem. A second mechanic, also in Udaipur, identified dirty points, and although it seemed to run better for a while, the problem still returned. A third mechanic outside Mount Abu thought the points needed resetting, but that made no difference whatsoever. I wasn't too worried, though, as I was going to one of the largest cities in India – Ahmedabad – where I knew I'd be able to get a complete service at the official Enfield dealership.

Ahmedabad is a big industrial city with *unbelievable* congestion in its streets, which make even those of Delhi look almost deserted. Once you've joined a group of moving vehicles, it's almost impossible to leave the flow. There's not even any room to pull over to consult a map.

On my way to the Enfield dealership I got completely lost and had to ask for directions.

I noticed a man in his thirties, wearing an unfeasibly white shirt (given the pollution), walking down the street.

'Excuse me!' I shouted through my full-face helmet, 'Does this road go to Gandhi Memorial?'

'Gandhi Memorial? I go there. I go with you,' he said, and climbed onto the back of my bike before I could stop him.

As I followed his instructions, we spoke.

'Where are you from?' he asked.

'England.'

'What is your good name?'

'Michèle. And what's your name?'

He told me his name and added, 'Are you a man or a

woman?'

'A woman.'

That seemed to silence him, so I concentrated on manoeuvring my bike through the traffic. After a while, I noticed he'd moved forward on the seat and was now pressing against me. I shuffled forward to get a bit of distance between us. A few seconds later he moved in closer again and was now squeezing my bum with his thighs. Again I moved forward, by this point almost straddling the fuel tank. But still he pressed against me. Finally, exasperated, I slammed on the brakes and ordered him off the bike.

'Okay, that's as far as I take you!' I declared. 'I'll find Gandhi Memorial on my own.'

'But it is still far,' he protested.

'I don't care. Just get off the bike right now. NOW!'

I eventually found the Enfield dealer. The manager promised to give the bike a complete check-up and have it ready by 6pm. In the meantime I took an auto-rickshaw to the beauty parlour used by his wife, where I had another of those complete pamperings consisting of a haircut, a massage, a manicure and a pedicure, for next to nothing.

When I returned to the garage the mechanic was putting the finishing touches on the service: he was cleaning the bike. He told me the cause of my problem had been a dirty carburettor. I wasn't convinced since it had only recently been cleaned.

I also asked the mechanic to adjust the front brake, but rather than tighten each of the three points separately, he simply tightened the cable on the handlebar so much that the front wheel could no longer turn freely. Since this was one of the things I'd learned from the Yorkshireman in Dharamsala, I ended up teaching the mechanic how to do it.

And to top it off, when he tried to repair the side indicators he managed to short-circuit some wires and had to replace the fuse.

By then I had serious doubts about the quality of his

workmanship, but I decided to ride back to my hotel 20km away as it was already 8pm. I was barely out of the town when the bike stalled. It continued to stall every few kilometres all the way back to my hotel: the journey took me over two hours. I was furious. The mechanic had only made the problem worse.

In the morning I rode – with difficulty – back to the Enfield dealer and complained. 'I'm not happy with the service I received yesterday,' I told him. 'It took eight hours for my bike to be serviced and I got it back in worse condition than before. And this is from an Enfield dealer,' I added, 'not from some scooter mechanic on the side of the road!'

'I am sorry madam. He is a new mechanic and he is still learning.'

The dealer got on the phone and spoke rapidly in Gujarati, but at one point he switched to English and said, 'I want this customer to leave fully satisfied.'

He hung up and turned to me. 'I have asked the best mechanic in Ahmedabad to look at your bike. You will not be charged for any parts since the guarantee is still valid, and I will not charge for the labour. I am very sorry about what has happened.'

The rest of the day was spent in a small workshop by the river in the town centre, watching an old man who didn't speak any English work on my bike. He moved slowly but with confidence. He checked the points, the carburettor, the tappets, and eventually, after six hours of work, he identified a damaged part: a small rip in the rubber tube to the air filter.

A little boy was sent out to buy a replacement and returned two hours later (!). With a new tube the bike ran a bit better, but it was still stalling regularly.

The mechanic decided to stop for the day, and I returned early the next morning. While he resumed his search for the problem, I decided to take a walk in the nearby streets of this run-down quarter of Ahmedabad.

I stopped by a shoe polish man squatting on the

pavement. In front of him he'd placed a row of small bottles of polish: red, black, white and ochre. From these he could create just about any shade of shoe leather.

My boots were very dirty and I decided to have them cleaned. The man placed a sheet of plastic on the ground for me to sit on while I removed my boots. I sat watching him work and admired the look of intense concentration on his lined face as he cleaned, waxed and polished. For just a few rupees, my boots looked almost new.

Then something strange happened that was to be repeated many times, in various forms, during my year-long trip. Seeming not to realise that to put the boot on I'd need the laces undone, after shaking the dust out of the laces and wiping them with a damp cloth he threaded them up all the way to the top of the first boot and tied a beautiful knot. Then he offered me the boot.

Amused, I took it from him, undid the laces and put it on. Was that a moue of displeasure around his mouth? He repeated the process with the second boot and again showed some annoyance when I undid his work.

When I returned to the mechanic he was all smiles. He'd found the problem: a faulty ignition coil. The boy was sent out and returned, again two hours later, with a replacement.

A test ride confirmed he had indeed solved the problem. I was thrilled – and he looked even more thrilled. I tried to pay him but he refused, indicating that the dealer would be paying him. He wouldn't even accept a soft drink, and instead insisted on buying *me* one.

Much happier now that Big Thumper was running well, I made my way down to Diu – a beach resort described as a 'quieter Goa'. It also had the added attraction that, unlike the rest of Gujarat, the purchase of alcohol was legal.

I broke off my journey at the Velavadar National Park, where I stayed in a lodge on the reserve and once again was the only guest. That seemed to be the pattern whenever I left the major towns.

I drove through the park both at sunset and sunrise to see the wildlife. I saw male and female blue bulls (they look like a cross between deer and cattle) that can live without water for long periods of time even in high temperatures. I also saw three large herds of blackbucks: a type of antelope of which the male has distinctive spiralled horns. I spotted pallid harriers, which are migratory birds from Europe, and – best of all – a female lesser florican. This bird looks a bit like a peacock, and there are only around 1,500 of them surviving in India. Approximately 80 of them come to this park during the mating season, but no one knows where they go after that.

I continued towards Diu, stopping for a few hours at the Alang ship-breaking yard that stretches for 10km along the seafront. Although only set up in 1982, it is now the biggest ship-breaking yard in the world. Its commercial success is due mainly to the low cost of employing the 50,000 workers who risk their lives every day to pull apart enormous ships – often literally by hand. At least 20 workers die every year through accidents, and some years it's more than 100.

I met a plot manager who spoke very good English and proudly showed me the two Russian destroyers he was in the process of dismantling.

'The workers are very skilled and come from far to work here,' he said.

'Where do they come from?' I asked.

'Bihar, Orissa and Utter Pradesh.'

Those are among the poorest states in India.

'They come here because of the high wages,' he explained. 'They can make as much as 100 rupees a day.'

Three dollars.

'Do they work both day and night?' I asked, having heard that the yard never stopped working.

'No, no. They work only fourteen hours every day. After that they go sleep and eat in the housing provided by the company.' He pointed to the endless rows of shacks where the 50,000 men – some with their families – lived.

'Can you explain to me what happens when a new boat comes in?' I asked.

He hesitated. 'You asking so much questions. Are you a journalist?'

'No,' I laughed. 'I love boats. That's why I'm interested.'

'Alright.' He pointed to an old P&O passenger cruiser that was anchored out at sea. 'The boats sail in with a minimum crew. And they stop as close to the beach as possible. The crew leaves the boat and go home or to their next job. Now the boat is ours. At high tide, we bring the ship to just 50 metres from the shore.

'Then we strip everything. You see the small boat coming from the big boat?' he asked me.

It was carrying gas cylinders. 'Yes,' I answered.

'That's how we bring the things into shore. We put it in the boats and bring it here to the beach.'

He pointed to various heaps on the sand. 'You can see we have different qualities of steel, we have cabling, wood, gas cylinders, wire netting. Everything is sold by weight. We also have furniture. Did you see it when you came to the yard?'

Indeed I had. On the road to the shipyard I'd passed what looked like the world's largest garage sale. For over three kilometres, all I could see were neatly arranged piles of plates, cups, chairs, bed-frames, mattresses, curtains, towels, telephones, fridges, washing machines, doors, sinks, toilets, fans and wall lamp fixtures.

The plot manager went on to explain that the workers then cut through the empty hull with gas-powered blow torches – first into large steel plates that were brought onto shores and then into smaller pieces that were sold for scrap.

~~~~~~~~~~

This is what the Indian tourist bureau writes about Diu:

'Diu, a beautiful blend of sun, sand and sea, is God's

gift to those in quest of a blessed turf where the weary weight of this unintelligible world can, for a while, be lightened and the waking soul can hear the music of the spheres.'

With this in mind, I expected great things. Unfortunately, the first day started off rather badly when I couldn't open up my new padlock on my bike. I'd bought the lock the day before but hadn't realised that the key didn't match it. Maybe to some people it's obvious that you need to check a key matches a padlock, but not to me.

I spent an hour going from hardware store to hardware store, growing more and more despondent as I was told I'd have to go to the nearest town on the mainland, 20km away, to find a locksmith. My final attempt was with the scooter mechanic, who lent me a hacksaw. I was pleased – but also worried – to discover how easy it was to saw through the lock.

While I was at the garage I met the mechanic's brother, who worked at London's Heathrow airport. He was only able to do this because residents of Diu could, prior to 1961, apply for Portuguese nationality and hence now benefitted from European Union membership. The older population still spoke Portuguese.

Despite the bad start to my stay in Diu, I had to agree with the tourism bureau that this island provided its visitors with a very relaxing interlude: the pace was gentle, the beaches deserted, the sea calm and the sea food delicious. My week in Diu felt like a holiday from my holiday; my main activities were lying on the beach and eating great meals. I came across some tourists who'd been here for six weeks already. It would be easy to do...

I met a civil servant in his mid forties, and his wife, in Diu's marketplace. The couple lived 300km away in Ahmedabad and had come for a short break, leaving their children with their grandparents. I was reading a newspaper and asked them to explain some of the various political parties fighting for the elections.

The man answered, 'I'm fed up with elections. We're

not really interested in all that; we prefer the simple life. These politicians, they make fun of us.'

When I asked him if he was going to vote he said yes, but that he hadn't yet made up his mind who for; he wanted to see which candidates the parties would field, and then he'd decide whether each candidate was 'a good man.'

He complained that politics was corrupt: 'Politicians are only after the money they can earn when they are in power. They don't care about the people. They don't care about our welfare. And if it looks like their party is losing popularity, the politicians just change parties, or create new ones.'

~~~~~~~~~~

'Puff!... Puff!'

I tried to stop only every 500 steps to catch my breath.

I'd counted 2,852 steps so far; how many more to make a total of 10,000? That's the number of steps to the top of Girnar Hill, a long day's ride from Diu, with its Jain and Hindu Temples.

I should have started at dawn, like everybody else, when it was cooler. But instead I started climbing at 10am when most people were already coming down.

Every time someone came down, they smiled and spoke to me. Always the same questions.

'What is your name?'

'Puff!... Michèle.... Puff!'

'What is your country?'

'Puff!... England.... Puff!'

If I wasn't quick enough they'd also ask which city. The answer would then usually elicit the exclamation, 'Oh, London proper!'

It does get rather annoying – especially after the first few dozen times (and the first few thousand steps).

Most of the people were families and children on school outings. There were also some old people and some ill people, hoping this pilgrimage would bring them relief. The most moving sight was a couple leading their blind daughter slowly down each step. She also had a clubfoot. Despite the effort, she smiled broadly and grunted at each step. Her parents had a patient, loving but pained look on their faces; they stopped by each beggar lining the route to donate a few rupees.

~~~~~~~~~~~~~

Back on the road again, I headed to the north of Gujarat. After a long day I treated myself to a good meal in the town of Rajkot, in one of the top restaurants recommended in my guidebook. Although there were some empty tables, I approached one with a red-faced, middle-aged Western man.

'Do you mind if I join you?' I asked.

'Of course not. I'm glad for a bit of female company.'

'Are you from New Zealand?' I asked.

'No. I'm Australian,' he replied. 'Do I look like a bloody sheep shagger?' He leaned over and added with a sly grin, 'So you didn't fancy eating with those bloody Indians then? Hehe. Can't say I blame you. Or was it my general good looks? Hehe.'

Shit, I thought. Maybe this wasn't such a good idea after all.

I smiled. 'No, I just fancied a conversation. I've been on the road and haven't really spoken to anybody for a while.'

'Oh! So you just want my conversation then, not my body. Oh well, too bad.'

He chewed on a chapati. 'Okay, let's have a conversation. Maybe you'll change your mind later about my body. Haha. So what do you think about India?'

Strange question, I thought. I usually only got it from Indians.

I answered, 'I'm having a great time here; I love it. It's such an adventure – even with all the hassle, I…'

He interrupted me. 'Yeah, all that bloody hassle. I can't wait to get out of here. I'm sick and tired of them Indians. Always asking for money. You can't trust any of them.'

His beer bottle was now empty and he bellowed across the room, 'Another beer!'

'Oh, you've had bad experiences, then?' I asked.

'Bad experiences? Every bloody *day* here is a bad experience,' he replied. 'One day they try to cheat you, another day they try to poison you. And to top it off they're all so bloody stupid. Honestly, have you met a smart Indian?'

'Well, actually...'

'No,' he jumped in, 'there aren't any.'

The waiter approached our table with a beer.

The Australian continued, 'Don't you find that the Indians are stupid?'

The waiter poured the beer, bowed slightly and walked away.

'I think he heard you,' I said.

'I don't bloody care. He's probably too stupid to understand.'

An Indian family at a table nearby turned around to look at us, and I looked down: guilty by association.

Smiling, one of the diners asked my companion, 'Which is your country, sir?'

'Czechoslovakia,' he lied.

'Surely you mean the Czech Republic, sir?'

India 1 – Foreigners 0.

~~~~~~~~~~

My next destination was a nature reserve in an area called the Little Rann of Kutch. There, I befriended another guest – an Indian man called Vijay who invited me back to his home for lunch in nearby Ahmedabad. I had planned on only riding through Ahmedabad as I'd already visited a couple of weeks earlier, but in the end I stayed for five days. Initially I expected Vijay to make a pass at me, but although we became very good friends and confided many of our thoughts, he never did. Instead he treated me as a friend and confidante. He was very interested in the world outside India and enjoyed discussing English literature – about which he knew much more than I did.

His house, in a walled complex of a few hundred luxury villas, was built on two levels with separate servant quarters. Vijay had lived with his wife, in this, his parents' home, but they had now separated and she'd gone back to her family. He now lived with just his mother and father, but I saw little of them as they occupied a different floor and seemed to have very different schedules.

While Vijay spent his days at work, I used his computer and internet connection to communicate with my friends and family back home. The servants periodically came up to check if I wanted another glass of iced tea or a snack. They even washed the dust off my bike whenever I took it out.

When Vijay returned from work we'd have a glass of Indian rum – despite the prohibition rules in the state – before going out for dinner with his friends in town.

Vijay's social group was totally fluent in English. In fact they spoke it better than they spoke Gujarati, even though they'd done all their schooling in India. I was introduced to a professional cricket player, a designer of western fashion and a business consultant.

Evenings went on until late, glasses were constantly replenished and the conversation revolved around the latest political scandals, business deals and Booker Prize winners.

As I sat on a beautiful white leather sofa, I reflected that rural Indians would find these fast-living, fast-talking Indians almost as strange as they found me.

For New Year' Eve, Vijay organised a party in his home and invited forty of his friends. I had nothing suitable to wear and so I bought a tight pair of jeans at Benetton and borrowed one of Vijay's white shirts, which

I tied about my shrinking waist. I danced until four in the morning to the tunes of ABBA and Queen, and drank lots of rum. No-one mistook me for a man.

The next day, as we nursed our hangovers, Vijay spoke to me about his family. His father's family had owned rice and sugar plantations in Burma, and had lived there for three generations. During the Second World War, his father, aged 13, had fled the Japanese and made his way to Bombay where he worked as a coolie in the railway station for four years. He then got a job working for a pasti-wallah (a person who deals in second-hand books and newspapers) and educated himself by reading books in the shop. From there he found a job as a clerk in an insurance company, and eventually set up his own business trading cotton in Yemen.

When the Korean War erupted and disrupted the normal trading routes, he made his fortune − which he promptly lost when the war ended. He became an employee again, and was eventually promoted to finance director of one of the biggest corporations in India. Not bad for a kid who started out as a railway porter.

Vijay's mother was also a businesswoman, whose small physique belied a very strong personality. In addition to her normal job in an insurance company, she spent an hour every morning trading petrochemical products on the phone before going to the office. She acted as a middleman between suppliers and consumers.

On the second morning of my stay I was summoned to her quarters. I sat in her bedroom with a cup of tea and watched her wheel and deal on the telephone while she lay on her bed. Although the conversation was in Gujarati, it was obvious from her voice that she was a tough negotiator and didn't waste time.

After hanging up the phone she looked up and questioned me about my job, my trip, and my personal life. After a few minutes it became clear that she was really trying to find out how long I'd be staying and what my intentions were regarding her son. I reassured her that I would soon be moving on, and that my friendship with Vijay was purely platonic.

Vijay, like both his parents, was a very high achiever and an entrepreneur. Whilst still at university he'd started selling computers and then set up a business selling office equipment. He'd just bought his partner out by borrowing from business friends in exchange for post-dated cheques. He assured me that this is a common way of doing business in India.

The morning of my departure, I sat at breakfast with Vijay and his mother and noticed a heavy atmosphere and a lot of murmuring between the two servants in the kitchen. I asked Vijay if something was happening.

He explained, 'We just heard that our housekeeper's brother has been kidnapped. He's the driver for one of the biggest businessmen in Ahmedabad.'

'How did it happen?' I asked.

'We don't know exactly. Our housekeeper just heard this morning on the telephone. The police found the car abandoned at one of the major roundabouts in the city centre. They think the businessman, his driver and his bodyguard were kidnapped at gunpoint from there.'

'What's going to happen now?' I asked.

Vijay replied, 'Well, it depends whether the kidnap was for ransom or to get rid of a business rival. If it's to get rid of a business rival then they could end up dead. If it's for a ransom, it'll probably get paid and they'll all reappear in a few days.'

'Which one do you think it is?'

'I don't know, I hope it was done for money.'

I later learned that the prisoners were eventually freed.

Chapter 10
Never depend on the placidity of cows

'Hello stranger!' an Australian voice shouted at me as I sat in the garden of my hotel outside Dhar, resting after a long couple of days' riding from Ahmedabad.

I thought, Oh, no! The Australian bigot from that restaurant in Rajkot has caught up with me!

With apprehension, I turned towards the source of the voice... and was pleasantly surprised to come face-to-face with Greg and Jess – the Australians I'd met the day of my accident two months previously and 4,000km away.

'I can't believe it!' I exclaimed as I hugged them. 'What are you doing here? Last time I saw you two, you were waving goodbye to me in the snow! I thought you were going to sell your bike in Delhi and go off to Thailand?'

Greg answered, 'We were having such a great time that we decided to stay in India instead. Besides, we didn't want to leave our Enfield just yet.'

Jess added, 'Also, our friend Mike decided to come to India and get himself a bike too. So we thought we'd stay and travel with him down south. Greg and I are going back to Oz in a couple weeks.'

They introduced me to Mike – a very tall, thin and good-looking man with a bone-crushing handshake.

Hmm... rather nice, I thought.

'How did you find me?' I asked.

Jess answered, 'When we checked in last night at our hotel, we met this guy who told us there was a woman staying here also riding an Enfield. We guessed it might be you, and this morning we looked at your bike.' She added, laughing, 'Still have those dents from the accident, heh?'

We decided to go and explore the fort town of Mandu and its fifteenth-century Afghan palaces. The men walked ahead, while Jess and I followed behind.

'So, who's Mike?' I asked her.

'He's a friend of ours from Melbourne. He's going to stay in India for a few months.'

'He's a bit quiet, isn't he?' I observed.

Jess explained, 'He just broke up with his girlfriend and decided a biking trip in India would be a good way to get over it.'

'Oh! So he's a wounded soul then, is he?'

'A bit. Although I think he knew it was over a long time ago. Anyway,' Jess added as she turned to me, 'why are you asking? Interested, are you?'

I laughed. 'I suppose I've always kind of liked the tall, quiet types.'

Jess asked, 'What about the boyfriend back home, then?'

'Oh! That's definitely over.'

'Does he know it?'

'Well, not in so many words – although I think he knew it before I left to come here.' I paused. 'Still, I suppose I really should call him and tell him.' I grimaced. 'Shit, I hate making those phone calls!'

'I don't think anybody likes making them,' Jess observed.

Later that day, I called Matthew in London.

After a bit of desultory chit-chat, I got to the point: 'Look, I know we said we'd see how we felt about each other when I came back, but... I've been thinking and... and I don't think I want to pick up where we left off.'

Matthew just listened, as usual.

'Matthew? Are you there?'

'Yes.'

'Look, I'm sorry...' I started...

'Actually, Michèle,' he interrupted, 'I can't say I'm surprised. And anyway, things have been happening for me here too...'

'Oh, I see.' I said.

'Yep. But I'd still like to hear from you,' he added.

'Send me e-mails!'

'Yes of course... Well, bye then.'

He hung up.

I didn't know it then, but his new girlfriend was already two months pregnant.

~~~~~~~~~~

The next few days were spent sightseeing around the forts with my Australian friends and trying to flirt with Mike. I wasn't sure whether he was responding, although he did give me a few meaningful looks across the dining table.

Anyway, we would soon be going our different ways. Jess and Greg wanted to go down to Goa as soon as possible because they needed to sell their bike before flying on home, and Mike would accompany them there and then stay on in Goa for a little while.

I, on the other hand, wanted to ride through to the Ajanta caves and Mumbai before heading to Goa. Since Mike knew exactly where he'd be staying, he suggested I meet him there in a couple of weeks.

I said goodbye to the three of them and set off alone on my bike, feeling a bit low. I knew I'd miss their company and I wondered if I would in fact meet up with Mike. I might not make it in time, or he might've decided to move on.

For a couple of hours I rode with a preoccupied mind. The road was in excellent condition, with hardly any potholes, and I was riding at 60km per hour with no other vehicles in sight. I could see two white cows ahead, on the other side of the road, facing away from me and standing still. However, as I approached them, one of the cows suddenly jumped around and galloped right across my path. It was being mounted by what was now very obviously a bull.

In general, the cattle in India move along at a very leisurely pace, but this cow's desire to avoid the bull's amorous embrace gave it a speed you wouldn't think possible. Although I managed to brake and swerve away from its body, the front of my bike collided with its horns. I fell over, hit my head on the ground and got trapped under the bike.

Almost immediately, two men emerged from a couple of shacks along the road and ran up to lift the bike. They could see I was dazed and didn't try to get me to sit up or take off my helmet. I lay on the side of the road, rocking myself. My knee was killing me. *Oh no!* Was this the end of my trip?

A minute or so later, as the pain started to subside, I looked up. The two men had been joined by a group of around thirty more men and women.

Where had they all come from? Surely not all from the two shacks by the road?

After checking there were no dents in my helmet, I gingerly took it off and a murmur ran through the crowd. A woman said something to me, of which I only caught the word 'lady'. I didn't know if she was making an observation or asking a question, but I nodded. She smiled and squeezed my shoulder, as if telling me I was going to be fine.

Afraid of what I might find, I looked down at my knee resting in a pool of liquid. With relief I realised it was only oil from the engine. I could feel the knee swelling up, but I could also move it. At least it wasn't broken.

'Doctor?' I asked. 'Do you know where I can find a doctor?'

Nobody spoke English, but they understood the word 'doctor' and pointed to the village I'd just passed. Two men helped me up and I hobbled to the other side of the road leaning on their shoulders. They stopped a tractor and I climbed onto it. What had seemed like a smooth road when I was on the bike now felt like a dry river bed: I could feel its every imperfection deep into my knee.

After a kilometre we reached the village and my two helpers half-carried me to the doctor's clinic, 100 metres from the road. The closer we got to the clinic, the bigger the crowd around me became. Fortunately, the doctor's room was so small that only a dozen spectators managed to squeeze in with me. The other two dozen stood by the door and outside the window, peering in.

As I cautiously pulled up my trouser leg for the doctor – and everyone else – to see, I thought to myself it was a good thing it was only my knee that was hurt.

My biggest fears were unfounded: I wasn't seriously hurt, and my knee was only quite badly grazed and a bit swollen.

As the doctor cleaned it with alcohol, I screamed, 'OUCH!'

My audience laughed.

The doctor then took out an old syringe to give me a tetanus injection.

'NO!' I cried out again, 'I don't need a tetanus shot. I had one before I came to India.'

I think he understood, but my giggling audience didn't. Obviously they thought me too chicken to have an injection. Too right!

Once bandaged up, I hitched another ride on a tractor with my two helpers to get back to my bike. The people from the shacks had kept guard over it and they helped me with the repairs. The only thing preventing my bike from running was a damaged accelerator cable, which we sorted out with a bit of string. The other damage – a bent leg frame, broken side mirror and broken front brake bracket – could wait until I got to the mechanic in Ajanta, just 25km away.

Once in Ajanta, another doctor examined me to make sure there was no concussion.

He asked, 'How did the accident happen?'

'Well, I was riding the bike when...'

I stopped myself. In view of the sacred status of cows, maybe I shouldn't tell him I'd almost killed a couple – nor what they were doing.

I continued, '...when a truck coming from the other side overtook a bullock cart and forced me off the road onto the gravel shoulder. I skidded and fell over.'

'Oh, yes, you must be careful with those truck drivers,' the doctor observed, sympathetically.

I rested for a couple of days in Ajanta and took my bike to the mechanic for repairs. The man didn't speak any English, but fortunately Indians use the English words for most of the bike parts. I explained that there were two things I wanted him to do:

- One: change the brake bracket
- Two: change the mirror

Most mechanics, I think, would have realised that although I listed them in that order, they should be done the other way around (you need to take off the brake bracket to get to the mirror, so you might as well change the mirror first).

But no. He took me literally and changed the brake bracket first. I tried to stop him, but my Hindi wasn't good enough. Eventually I gave up and watched his face as he finished with the bracket and realised he'd have to take it off again to get to the mirror bracket. But rather than being embarrassed by his mistake, he glared at me as if I'd misled him.

My fault for giving him instructions in that order.

After getting my bike fixed I visited the 1,500-year-old Ajanta caves, famous for their Buddhist paintings and statues. Each cave is carved out of the mountain and provides a cool, dark refuge from the glaring heat outside. I wandered around in quiet contemplation – until a large but silent group of schoolchildren appeared and then a horde of rambunctious soldiers tore through the place. It was curious to see the children walking hand-in-hand, two by two in an orderly line, while the soldiers ran around, shouting and climbing onto the statues.

~~~~~~~~~~

My next destination was Bombay (or as it has been renamed, Mumbai), which I approached with some trepidation. Many Western tourists, when I'd spoken to them about it, had only disparaging things to say: filth, traffic, poverty, noise, etc.

So it came as a surprise that, to me, Mumbai seemed a respite from India. Of course, there were the crippled beggars, the cows meandering through the streets and the unbelievable traffic jams, but what I remember most was seeing young Indian women wearing skirts so short they'd turn people's heads – even in the West.

If I'd come straight from London it probably would've been the beggars that stuck in my mind, but Mumbai surprised me with its air-conditioned offices supplied with the latest computer technology, and thrilled me with its shops. A highlight was buying French bread and cheeses and having a picnic in my hotel room. All I was missing was red wine – though I'm sure that could've been arranged.

I stayed in Mumbai for five days doing the usual tourist things, and then spent a couple of days riding down south to Goa to meet up with Mike.

Chapter 11
Raving in Goa

I was pleased to find Mike still in Goa, and judging by the strength of his hug it seemed he was also pleased to see me. We decided to take a walk on the beach as the sun set over the Arabian Sea.

As we watched the waves roll in onto the palm-fringed beach, Mike took my hand and said, 'I'm glad you decided to come – I wasn't sure if you would. I know I sometimes come across as pretty distant.'

'I understand,' I replied. 'Jess told me about your girlfriend back home.'

'Yeah, I was pretty cut up about it, but I'm getting over it now. It'd be good if you could stay a little while here,' he said as he gently kissed me.

Hurray! I thought. After almost four months on the road, finally a little bit of romance! And what better setting than the tropical paradise of Goa?

The next day I rushed out to buy myself a flowing summer dress. After all, a romantic adventure requires a romantic wardrobe. Also, it wouldn't do to be mistaken for a man while I walked hand-in-hand with Mike…

Many people have a very bad image of Goa as a modern beach resort full of package holidaymakers, spaced-out ravers and gawking Indian men; stories about bus tours of the beaches set up for Indian tourists who want to see topless Western women don't help, either. (So it goes, some coach companies even provide a money-back guarantee: 'no breasts, no charge.')

Instead I found Goa peaceful and easy-going, and even though there's obviously a foreign influence on the people – both through the Portuguese colonisation of the sixteenth century and the presence of Western tourists – the flavour remains very much Indian, especially if you venture just a few kilometres inland. The population is mainly Catholic, but although a lot of women wear skirts during the day, they put on their saris for Sunday church.

Mike and I stayed in Arambol, a tiny fishing village where in recent years many small pensions and restaurants had sprung up. A large number of village families also rented out their houses to tourists and moved in with other relatives during the high season in winter.

This was one of the quietest Goan resorts: it was only accessible by ferry across a river, and most of the foreigners staying there were 'old India hands' – some had been around for a few months, some for a few years. One woman I met had been there four years, doing not much of anything. (Her words, not mine.)

There was talk of a Japanese company trying to buy a large strip of land to build a hotel/golf club complex, but the locals were fiercely opposing this as they feared it would drain the scarce water resources and chase the budget tourists away – upon whom the poorer villagers relied for a living.

Although the beach was very beautiful and fringed with coconut palm trees, life here revolved less around lying on the sand and more around lazing about in the shade: not surprising with a temperature of 35 degrees celsius and 90% humidity...

Mike and I stayed in during the heat of the day and emerged in the late afternoon to watch the sunset, eat seafood, and drink a few cold beers in one of the many bars on the beach.

As well as its magnificent beaches and leafy country lanes, Goa is renowned for its party scene – especially techno. There's even a particular type of music known as 'Goan techno'. Despite living in London, I'd never been to a rave and so I was very curious to go.

Word was out that there was going to be a big outdoor party on the top of a plateau a kilometre out of the village. Since these things didn't get going until the early hours of the morning, Mike and I went to sleep for a couple of hours and then set off at 1am.

Barely out of our guesthouse, we met a very disappointed young ABBA lookalike, who even turned out to be Swedish. I don't know what I expected rave-goers to wear, but it certainly wasn't a silver halter top, blue eye-shadow and flared polyester trousers. This undoubtedly shows how badly out of touch I was.

The young woman told us in a despondent tone that, once again, the Goan police had come in and broken up the party. This was supposedly despite all the appropriate bribes having been paid to the authorities.

She complained, 'It's the fourth party I've had cancelled on me since I got to Goa. It's the last time I try. I give up.' She sat down on a low wall, dejected.

We went back to our guesthouse and back to sleep.

The next day, however, we were invited to a private techno party on the beach to celebrate the marriage of an Englishman to a Goan woman. Her brother also happened to be a police officer, so it was quite safe to assume that this party at least would not get busted.

It was a small-scale affair: no more than 30 people, almost exclusively Westerners, and there were very few women. Even the bride disappeared early in the evening.

The party appeared to be divided into two types of people: the Stoned and the High. The Stoned, dressed in brightly coloured but dirty cotton trousers and long shirts, sat quietly on the sand, smoking hash and swaying gently to the beat of the music. The High, dressed in baggy shorts and bare-chested, danced frenetically around the loudspeakers, their heads bobbing up and down, their arms swinging all over the place and their bodies glistening with sweat. Now and then, one would jump up to a table and drink copious amounts of water.

I joined the High (minus the bare chest) and danced until 5am, at which point we finally stumbled back to our guesthouse and spent the next day in a heavy-limbed stupor. Not that different to how I'd been feeling anyway, given the weather – but this time at least I had an excuse.

After a few more days of lazing about, Mike and I forced ourselves to venture out of the village and visit Old Goa, a city two hours away.

The town was dominated by three churches, built in the Tuscan style by the Portuguese over three hundred years ago. If it hadn't been for the Indians inside the churches, they could have been in the middle of Italy. One of the churches, the Basilica of Bom Jesus, contained a rather ghoulish site: the preserved body of the missionary St Francis Xavier, who died in 1552. Originally the plan had been to bury him in Goa, but the faithful noticed that – despite a long journey from China, where Francis had died – the body was not decomposing, and a miracle was declared.

Rather than bury this wonder, the body was kept in the church where Christians could venerate it properly. Unfortunately, some were so taken by the body that they started taking it apart; and various limbs and organs ended up spread all over the world, as far as Italy and Japan. Eventually, what was left of the body had to be placed in protective glass casing high up in the nave and only brought down to eye-level every ten years.

At the previous showing, in 1995, over one million pilgrims had come to view the body. However, we didn't need to wait until 2005 to see this miracle: Mike and I were wandering on the second level of the monastery adjacent to the church when he noticed a half-opened wooden door; he stuck his head through and found himself on a little balcony directly over the open tomb in the church. Although the monastery was open to the public, and there were no signs barring our entry through that door onto the balcony, I had no doubt we were not meant to be there. If pilgrims had to wait 10 years for a glimpse of the saint, I was sure tourists weren't meant to sneak a preview like that. Suddenly afraid we'd get charged with desecrating a religious site, we quickly exited the monastery.

Just for the record: the body may be preserved but it is

certainly very desiccated.

~~~~~~~~~~~

My relationship with Mike, though pleasant, was coming to an end. We'd vaguely talked about travelling together for a little while, but I had misgivings about it. How could I fit him into the lone-biker-chick-with-her-trusted-mount script I had running through my head? I knew I'd soon start relying on his mechanical skills; and though the trip might've become safer and less lonely, it would also have become less exciting. In the end, he was quite happy to stay while I set off on my own.

With the hot season quickly approaching, I wanted to visit Karnataka, Kerala and Tamil Nadu. It was the end of January now, and by March the heat would be excruciating – forty-five plus degrees being quite common.

Unlike the locals – many of whom wore knitted sweaters in thirty-degree temperatures – I felt the heat and was no longer able to ride the bike wearing my leather jacket. Instead I wore a long-sleeved shirt with the cuffs tucked into my riding gloves: another good reason to avoid falling off Big Thumper.

Chapter 12
Philosophising in Karnataka

The town of Badami was the capital city of the Chalukyan Empire 1,300 years ago; now it was just a small, quiet provincial town nestled inside a red sandstone canyon and surrounded by dilapidated Hindu, Jain and Buddhist temples.

As I parked my bike alongside one of the temples, set by a tranquil lake where young girls were washing laundry, I was assailed by a dozen little boys who insisted on escorting me into the building. There they demonstrated the acoustics by singing the French nursery rhymes 'Alouette, gentille alouette' and 'Frère Jacques.' Although the boys had no trouble with the melodies, the words had changed beyond recognition. I tried to join in but they kept on correcting my pronunciation and seemed surprised I didn't know the words. (For the record, I was brought up in France and I do know the words.)

Once they'd finished their recital they asked me to teach them an English song, and all I could come up with was 'Jingle Bells', which I realise was probably not very appropriate in a Hindu temple. Still, they seemed to like it and sang the song on the steps of the temple with full gusto and a lot of laughter.

Later I climbed up the canyon to visit some cave temples known for their stone-carved statues. The figures were very intricate and the representations of the male gods anatomically correct.

A group of schoolchildren from the nearest major town was also visiting the statues. They were obviously fascinated by the sights. The girls pretended not to look at the male forms, but I could see them peeking shyly out of the corner of their eyes while the boys giggled and nudged each other. One of the boys had a water bottle and, clearly feeling brave, he ran around the cave splashing water between the statues' legs and then ran out shrieking with laughter.

~~~~~~~~~~

My next destination was Hampi – another city famed for its temples – 150km away from Badami. I decided to avoid the national highway as I'd learned by now that 'national highway' doesn't necessarily mean a road thats's wide or in good condition. What it does mean is trucks, and lots of them.

Before I left in the morning, my hotel manager suggested an alternative route via some minor roads, and wrote down the names of the villages I'd have to go through. He wrote them in both English and the local script of Kannada so that I could show the piece of paper when asking for directions. This was a trick I'd often use, since my pronunciation of the names of towns hadn't improved. The only problem then, of course, was to find someone who looked likely to be literate, since the average literacy rate was only 50% in India – and probably even worse in these rural areas.

It was best to avoid women and old men. A good bet was a young man on a scooter; he was likely to be well-off and therefore better educated. Even better was a pharmacist.

At one of my many stops for directions, a young man asked me to take him to his town 20km away. My first reaction was to refuse, remembering the experience I'd had with my last male passenger who'd pressed himself against me far more than the road conditions had warranted.

However, since this young man seemed inoffensive and rather shy, I agreed. 'Okay, but I'm a lady.' I pointed to the back of the seat. 'You sit here and I sit there far away from you, in front. And no touching, okay?'

He laughed. 'No problem, no touching!'

He was as good as his word and never touched me during the half-hour ride to his home. I deposited him in front of his house, but as I pulled off, the bike's clutch cable broke.

The young man offered to help: 'The mechanic is not far. We can push the bike there.'

As we pushed the bike the hundred metres down the street we acquired a following of dozens of young men who escorted us all the way to the mechanic.

The garage was empty except for a little boy sitting on the floor.

'Hello,' I said, 'where is the mechanic?'

The little boy got up and smiled.

'You speak English?' I enquired.

He approached my bike and had a short conversation with my hitchhiker.

Then, turning to me, the young boy asked, 'You have spare clutch cable?'

'Yes, here it is,' I said as I handed it over. 'Is the mechanic coming?'

He squared his shoulders and replied, 'I am the mechanic.'

This boy did not look more than ten years old.

He picked up his tools and walked over to my bike. In under ten minutes he'd replaced the cable.

However, it took me another fifteen minutes to get away from his garage, due to the attention of a group of over 60 onlookers. It was market day, and the word must have spread that there was a Western woman on a bike at the mechanic's.

I was bombarded with questions from all sides.

'What is your country?'

'What is your good name?'

'Are you married?'

'What is your profession?'

'You like our India?'

'You travelling alone?'

A young boy felt my biceps and gave me a big smile.

An older boy translated this to 'strong lady.'

Another boy was very impressed with my helmet and put it on his head. After that everybody else wanted to try it on, and each time one put it on, the whole crowd erupted in laughter.

Finally the helmet came back to me and I had their full attention as I fastened it. The crowd grew silent and I could feel them awaiting my kick-start. Would I manage to start the bike at the first attempt?

Phew! The bike started up and the crowd applauded. I revved the engine, gave a little wave, and rode off to enthusiastic cheers.

Hampi was everything the tourist guide had promised and more. I loved the setting of this village amongst the ruins of one of the largest and richest cities of the sixteenth century. In fact, after Peking, this had been the largest city in the world at that time, with half a million inhabitants. Now it was a sleepy town located in magnificent surroundings on the banks of the Tungabhadra river. I especially loved walking in the narrow ravine and jumping from boulder to boulder as the sun set.

~~~~~~~~~~

After visiting Hampi and its temples, I set off for Jog Falls around sunrise to avoid riding in the heat of the afternoon. However, after four hours of riding I felt very sleepy and needed to rest for a while. I found the ideal spot: a bed of leaves under a tree off the main road.

I parked the bike out of sight from the odd passing truck and dozed off, but only a few minutes later I woke up with a start: a shepherd was squatting only ten metres away from me, staring intently.

'Namaste,' I greeted him.

'Ball pen, ball pen,' he replied.

I was used to giving ball pens to children, but this was the first time I gave one to an adult – and a rather old one at that.

Holding the pen, the shepherd moved off to a nearby rock and crouched to look at me. Sleep was now out of the question, especially since his goats were now trying to get into my luggage.

I packed up and got back on the road. Half an hour later, I came across an overturned bus. I'd seen many wrecked vehicles on my travels, but it was clear this accident had only just happened: a small child was crying alongside two bodies, apparently thrown from the bus.

Another bus had stopped and people were running to the scene. Averting my eyes, I rode around the vehicle. I didn't want to see this: I'd heard too many stories of foreigners trying to help at the scene of an accident, only to find themselves spending a few days in jail under suspicion of having caused it, and only being released once a suitable bribe had been paid. Of course, these stories should be taken with a grain of salt. But in a warped way I was glad not to have any medical training: I could soothe my conscience by telling myself I couldn't have been of any help anyway. The truth is I was just scared.

~~~~~~~~~~~~

With a drop of over 250 metres, Jog Falls is the second-highest waterfall in India. After hiking down to the bottom, I went for a swim in the small lake formed by the cascades. I then lay on the boulders to dry in the sun, but I quickly covered up my very modest one-piece swimming costume as Indian teenagers gathered around to look.

I've seen Indian women swimming in lakes, and they go into the water fully dressed. The strange thing is that I've also seen women washing themselves in the local village lake, and there they're happy to remove their tops to soap themselves. Nudity seems acceptable – and studiously ignored – as long as the context is that of hygiene.

~~~~~~~~~~~~

As well as Hindus, this area of southern India (Karnataka) has a sizeable Christian minority. So far I'd met quite a few people with biblical names such as Zacharia, Lazarus and Joseph. However, I'd read in the paper that in some Christian areas in the north-east of India, the desire to give one's children foreign-sounding names had been taken to extremes. In fact, any name would do. The list of candidates in the upcoming elections included a Frankenstein W. Momin, a Lenin R. Marak, and a Stalin L. Nangmin. A current member of parliament was Adolf Hitler Lu Marak.

The article then proceeded to illustrate this strange tendency with the following two anecdotes:

An illiterate working-class couple went to the Pastor of the Presbyterian Church in Shillong, asking for their daughter to be named.

'What do you want your daughter to be named?' the priest asked.

'Presitue,' said the parents.

The bewildered priest asked the parents what the word meant.

'We have no idea, but it's an English name,' the parents replied.

In the other anecdote, a woman called First Gear had five children. The first four children – all sons – were called First, Second, Third and Fourth Gear, while the youngest, a girl, was named Back Gear.

~~~~~~~~~~~~

Mysore Palace is an Indo-European extravaganza that was built at the beginning of the nineteenth century. It contains an amazing mishmash of Belgian furniture, gilded mirrors, French bronze statues, English cast iron pillars, and paintings of Hindu deities that look just like Italian renaissance cherubs, all topped by a giant stained-glass dome with bright paintings of peacocks. Surprisingly, the overall effect is one of light and space.

Another thing that works in the palace's favour is the high standard of cleanliness and general upkeep: no signs of cockroaches, mould, chipped plaster, peeling paint, broken stairs or electrical wires hanging loose.

The ex-Maharaja still lived in a part of the palace, and I suspected the high level of maintenance was probably due to his presence. His father was the 25th and final Maharaja of Mysore, and the story of his death is quite interesting – albeit, in my opinion, rather implausible. The tale was told to me by one of the guards in the palace: in 1971, Indira Gandhi stripped all Indian Maharajas of their title and, more importantly, of their annual pension (Privy Purse). As a result, the 25th Maharaja could not pay for the upkeep of the palace and it became inevitable that the government would take possession of his home. He sunk into depression and, in 1974, killed himself by swallowing a crushed diamond – supposedly the favourite way for the aristocracy to commit suicide.

When I came out of the palace I walked straight into a political rally. The national elections were in two weeks and the tempo had been steadily rising. The crowd of a few thousand people seemed a happy one; some people were singing, some were chanting, and some were dancing. Some were also obviously drunk.

A few trucks, illuminated like Christmas trees, slowly moved with the demonstrators while Hindi pop blared out of their speakers. Every now and then an oversized cardboard representation of the head of a party leader would bob along the flow of people. The supporters were marching to the town's main square, where the local Congress candidate for the region was expected to make a speech at six o'clock in the evening (although when I left at seven thirty he still hadn't appeared).

While standing on the edge of the crowd, I started a conversation with a man in his thirties whose job was to paint giant billboards promoting upcoming films. He pointed to a wall on the other side of the road, advertising a Western film.

'I painted that.'

The chubby faces of the actors looked vaguely familiar, but it wasn't until I read the English script 'Airforce One' that I recognised Harrison Ford and Glenn Close. Both the male and female ideals of beauty are considerably more… let's say… *padded* in India than in the West.

Although the billboard artist was wearing a baseball cap with the insignia of the Congress party, he had no intention of voting for them. He told me he'd be voting for the BJP, which is the Hindu nationalist party, as he believed only it could create a strong and stable government for India. He also felt they should be given a chance to show what they could do.

'So why are you here, if you've already decided you're not voting for Congress?' I asked.

He smiled. 'The party will be giving me something for being here.'

'Like what?'

'Fifty or maybe one hundred rupees.'

That's a day's wage for most people.

He then added, pointing at the crowds, that a lot of the people this evening would also be receiving some kind of payment – in money or maybe food, or even alcohol.

I stayed another day in Mysore but found the rising heat difficult to cope with. For respite I decided to head for the Coorg region (also known as Kodagu), 100km west of Mysore. Although it's seldom visited by foreign tourists, this area is known for its green mountains, pleasant climate, fragrant coffee plantations and subdued pace.

Coorg is a small mountain district in the south-west of the state of Karnataka; at its longest it measures 100km, at its widest 60km. There are very few roads – originally to protect the province against invaders – or villages; instead people live in solitary houses or, if an extended family, in home-stays.

I stayed in the home of a local couple, Suresh and Sushila, in a house 45 minutes' walk (uphill, having left Big Thumper at the bottom of the track) from the road, set in acres of coffee shrubs, cardamon plants and pepper vines. Nearby were dense forests clinging onto the mountain slopes, and lowland jungles buried in isolated valleys from which tigers still emerged occasionally to hunt for cattle. Sushila complained that every year they lost four or five heads of cattle to the tigers.

The area is generally prosperous, and the people take pride in their gardens, where glorious poinsettia and bougainvillea decorate fences and walls. The climate is mild – never too far from 20 degrees celsius during the day – and the monsoon is very heavy and lasts over six months; although even that, Sushila assured me, is a beautiful time as everything glitters and mist rises from the jungle.

Tigers are protected in the area, and despite sightings being rare, I was still hoping to see one as I walked above the valleys and up to the highest mountain of Coorg (1,750m). During the hike I met up with four other Western foreigners who were resting on a promontory.

Suddenly, one of the women pointed at an animal on a far hill just by the edge of the forest: 'There's a strange-looking cow over there,' she said. 'Hang on, no... it's not a cow – it doesn't move like a cow. Oh my God, it's a tiger! Yes, it's a tiger!'

'Where? Where?' we cried.

She pointed with her finger, 'There, just there! By the trees. You see?'

There were lots of trees around. That's why it's called a forest. And where exactly was she pointing? That wasn't enough for me. It was, however, enough for two of the three other men, who joined the chorus.

'Yes! Oh my God, it's a tiger!' they exclaimed. 'It's moving towards the trees. Oh no! It's going under them. You can't see it anymore – it's gone under the canopy.'

Although I stared at the trees for another quarter of an

hour, willing the tiger to emerge, it didn't.

So the best I can say is that I stood next to people who saw a tiger. Or so they said…

~~~~~~~~~~

In the early nineteenth century, Coorg was ruled by King Veeraja: an extremely corrupt man. He ransacked the treasure coffers for his extravagant lifestyle, and fulfilled his sexual urges by kidnapping noble Coorgi women.

In addition, he was convinced – justly, as it turns out – that everyone was plotting against him, and anyone who fell under his suspicion was summarily executed – often by being impaled or crucified and left out to be eaten alive by vultures. Eventually he executed one too many people and his own ministers asked the British, who were already in a neighbouring state, to intervene. (At least that's what my British history book told me.)

And so, from 1834 until Indian Independence, Coorg was a protected state of the British Empire and allowed to retain a nominal independence. The British gave the Coorgis the unique right in India to carry weapons, and to this day the British are held in very high regard there. My host, Suresh, spoke very highly of the British and believed their popularity in the region was due to the fact that they never tried to subjugate Coorgi culture and impose their way of life or religion. As he put it, 'successful imperialism is one which respects local customs.'

Peter, an English psychologist on holiday, was also staying in their house. One evening, as we sat on the veranda watching the sunset, Peter suggested an interesting theory to explain the phenomenon I described as 'curious indifference': the Indian habit of staring at someone with what appears to be blank incomprehension.

Peter argued that Hinduism stresses the need for humans to fulfil their religious duties while accepting that they have little power over the external world – which anyway is a lot less interesting than the inner world.

'Therefore', he explained, 'it's not surprising that most Indians have little interest in, or comprehension of, your reasons for travelling in their country. To them, one should strive to explore one's inner world, not the outer world. To them, travelling and learning about other cultures is not interesting: it's a waste of time. Much better to spend your time exploring inside yourself. That's what'll give them a chance at a better reincarnation. They attach more value to the spiritual journey than to the physical journey.

'Also,' Peter added, 'Indian culture puts much less emphasis on the freedom of the individual than we do in the West. Here, the person is defined by the relationships he has with his family, his caste, his village. In the West we think there's a core inside us that's constant. We value individuality, integrity and personal need; while Indians value harmony between the person and the group, the person and the family. With such divergent views of what constitutes a person, Indians would find it difficult to understand why someone would apparently sever all personal relationships – which after all, they believe, define her personal nature – to travel alone in a country with which she has no links.'

Later on, it struck me that another fundamental difference between Hindus and Westerners is in their view of death. In the West, we fear death and seek to prolong life as long as possible. In contrast, although Hindus believe in reincarnation, they strive for release (they call it 'moksha') from the painful cycle of rebirth. Life is something to be endured rather than enjoyed: a successful Hindu life is one that achieves final annihilation – by good deeds and by doing one's duty without complaint – as opposed to the Western concept of a life that's full of excitement, love and the pursuit of knowledge (my definition). In that context it makes sense for the Westerner to be the one exploring the world, while the Hindu is the one *enduring* the world while exploring his spirituality.

~~~~~~~~~~~~

On the first day of the national elections in India, voting took place in 15 out of the 25 states. The second phase would take place the following week. I was curious to see the voting, so I rode with my hostess, Sushila, sitting side-saddle, to the nearest voting point.

The Coorg hills had a polling station every three kilometres so as to facilitate the process, since almost nobody had any transport. The polling booth was outside the village, in a small building that was usually used for weddings, engagements and naming ceremonies.

Sushila walked past an armed soldier and into the building while I waited outside on my motorcycle. A few minutes later she emerged with a government official.

'Would you like to see how we exercise democracy in India?' he asked me.

'I'd love to.'

'Come with me.'

I followed him back into the building to his desk, where he showed me a ballot paper. Since such a high proportion of the electorate was illiterate, the ballot paper consisted of the various party symbols alongside the names of the candidates. In this area there were six candidates: three independents, who had symbols of a boat, a manual water pump and a diesel water pump, as well as representatives of three national parties: Congress (a hand), BJP (a lotus flower) and Janata Dal (a wheel).

While I sat on the bench against the wall of this high-ceilinged room, an old lady dressed in a green cotton sari came in to vote. She shuffled up the wooden stairs into the large room and paused to catch her breath. Once rested, she fished out of her basket a pair of magnifying Buddy Holly glasses and approached the official's desk. He asked for her name, and a rather scruffy young man dressed in a dirty beige shirt and grey trousers confirmed her identity. Sushila explained this was to make sure no-one voted on her behalf.

Taking the blank ballot paper and seal that were offered to her, the woman slowly walked to a table on the far side of the room, upon which two cardboard boxes were placed. While hiding behind a box, she put her seal beside one of the candidates' symbols. Then she folded the paper and placed it in a locked metal box which was guarded by an armed soldier.

After voting, the disheveled youth marked the root of the old lady's index fingernail with black ink to ensure she only voted once. The ink would fade away after a month – unless she'd put vaseline on her finger, in which case it'd fade within a few hours with vigorous scrubbing, thus allowing the unscrupulous to vote again.

The seal used for voting is in the shape of a swastika with an arrow at the end of each branch. The swastika was originally a Hindu symbol ('swasti' means 'well-being' in Sanskit); Suresh, my host, explained that Hindus draw the symbol anti-clockwise, while Nazis draw it clockwise to represent Aryan purity.

'That may be so,' I noted, 'but why did I see it drawn clockwise in a Hindu temple only five kilometres from here?'

'Just a mistake,' replied Suresh.

Until a few years before, the ballot seal was simply a cross, but it had to be changed to something that was not symmetrical because, if the ink wasn't dry, the cross would get duplicated alongside another candidate's name when the ballot paper was folded, thus invalidating the vote. Now the person who counted the votes knew that the anti-clockwise swastika is the valid seal, not the clockwise one.

This is how the first day of the elections was reported in *The Deccan Herald*:

'The first phase of the... elections in 222 constituencies today passed off peacefully across the country... barring incidents of violence in Bihar, Andhra Pradesh and Assam where 22 people were killed. Eighteen people were killed in clashes, landmine blasts and shootouts in Bihar alone.'

There were also 'some 800 hundred complaints of booth capturing.'

If that's a *peaceful* election, I thought, let's hope the second phase isn't marred by violence.

After voting, Sushila took me to her coffee plantation where we picked coffee with her workers. It was good fun doing it for half an hour – although I doubt her workers thought so. There was no smell of coffee, but a wonderful sweet fragrance emanated from the white blossoms.

Then it was time to go home. I was determined to ride the bike all the way back to the house rather than park it at the beginning of the track; this was partly motivated by laziness since it was a hard 45-minute climb, and partly by pride. Not only did Suresh drive his jeep (with trailer) up the track every day, but a few years previously he'd go up the mountain on an Enfield 350cc with Sushila riding side-saddle on the back. If he can do it, I thought, so can I.

Wrong.

Big Thumper couldn't get a proper grip on the red dirt and loose stones. The more I tried, the louder the engine roared and the faster the back wheel spun. After a few minutes it became clear that Sushila would have to walk. A few minutes later still, it became clear that we would both have to walk.

I turned around and shakily went back down to park the bike, but even that was very difficult due to the steepness of the track and I fell over a few times. I'd obviously overestimated my riding skills.

~~~~~~~~~~~

One evening, over dinner, I asked Suresh about the position of women in Coorg.

He proudly replied, 'Coorgi women have a very high status here. Much higher than in the rest of India. We don't discriminate against widows here; they are not seen as impure. We encourage them to remarry.

'Also, when a woman marries we have a special ceremony to show how important she is in the family. During the ceremony, the bride takes out some cow dung from her husband's home and comes back in with a jug of water.'

I waited for the punchline, but none came.

I laughed, 'Suresh, call me a cultural imperialist, but that doesn't seem like much of an honour for the woman. She takes the shit out of the home and fetches water from the well!'

Taken aback, he thought for a few seconds, and then grinned. 'You're right: when you put it that way, it doesn't look like such a good job!'

Sushila, his wife, smiled gently and said nothing.

The next day, Sushila and I rode to a market town 25km away to attend the wedding of a friend of hers. The wedding celebrations were held in what I suppose would be called the town hall. Chairs had been set out in the main room, in rows facing a raised platform where the actual ceremony took place.

Although we arrived too late to see the ceremony, we timed it perfectly for the lunch and the musical entertainment in the shady courtyard. The bride and groom, however, did not join us. Instead they sat in separate rooms greeting guests.

We first went to see the groom, who was dressed all in white with a gold turban; Sushila wished him happiness and gave him an envelope containing money. In another room, the bride sat on a mattress on the floor with female relatives. She was dressed in a bright red sari and weighed down with so much gold it was just as well she was sitting down. She had gold rings on her toes and fingers, gold bracelets around her ankles and wrists, and gold earrings, nose ring and necklaces.

Lunch was a stand-up affair and quite similar to a wedding back home: lots of people milling around in their best clothes (at least in the case of the women), talking about their children and the quality of this year's coffee harvest, while a lone drunkard tried to join in the conversation and was politely ignored.

Chapter 13
Land's end

On the way out of the Coorg mountains, while heading towards the hot plains, I rode through the Nagarhole Wildlife Tiger Sanctuary, where I had trouble avoiding the potholes as my eyes were peeled on the undergrowth in the hope I'd finally see a tiger.

Instead, as I rounded a bend, I came face-to-face with a male elephant no more than 10 metres from the road. In panic, I braked. But when the elephant let out a big roar and took a couple paces towards me, I had the sense to accelerate away while also letting out my own big roar – of laughter and relief. I have no idea whether elephants charge motorbikes, but this was not the time to find out.

Two days later, while riding through another reserve (the Bandipur Wildlife Reserve), I learned that seeing an elephant was a lot easier than seeing a tiger. A herd of nine elephants – including two baby elephants – totally oblivious to my presence, slowly crossed the road in front of me. Still unsure as to whether they could prove dangerous, I decided against dismounting to get my camera out of my bag.

I was making my way to the Nilgiri Hills, at an altitude of over 2,000 metres; my trip to the south of India was turning into a journey in search of cooler mountain climes. And besides, it was a lot more fun riding the bike on quiet, shady, twisted mountain roads than on hot, dusty, busy coastal national highways.

I chose to stay in Kotagiri, a small hill station 30km away from the more famous British hill station called Ooty. It seemed every hill station I visited was once frequented by the British. Today, however, Kotagiri's economy revolves mainly around the growing of tea, and the business of running expensive boarding schools for the sons of the middle classes who live in the towns down in the plains.

It took me a couple of days to cover the 300km from the hill station to the town of Cochin on the coast, via the town of Coimbatore, which was made (in)famous only ten days previously when over 50 people were killed in a series of 14 bomb explosions linked to Muslim sectarianism and the national elections. Many tourists were avoiding the town, but I figured security was likely to be very tight. And anyway, since the voting had taken place three days before I arrived, there wouldn't be much point in planting bombs to influence the voters – assuming that had been the motive.

Security was indeed very tight, with the whole centre of town sectioned off, an armed soldier every 50 metres and checkpoints every half-kilometre. At one of the checkpoints I was stopped.

A soldier dressed in khaki, with a rifle over his shoulder, said something in the local language.

'Sorry, I'm a tourist,' I replied in English, 'I don't understand.'

He looked at my bike, now heavily laden with my bags. (I was over my obsession with travelling light by this stage.)

'Open your bags!' he ordered.

Oh, no, I thought. They're all locked up and chained up together; this could take a long time.

I decided to try another tactic instead. Pretending I'd misunderstood, I took off my helmet and, with a big smile, handed over my passport for inspection.

It worked, and after a quick look at my papers the soldier waved me through.

I then rode through unending tea plantations that looked very incongruous in the context of chaotic India: the endless hills, all the same size and equally spaced from each other, looked man-made. The tea bushes, of a green so bright they looked artificial, were kept neatly trimmed, and only the sight of the women tea-pickers in torn saris confirmed I was still in India. There were no emaciated cows, no swarms of flies, no piles of rotting litter, no smells of decomposing vegetation mixed with urine, no crumbling wooden shacks by the road, no dust, and not even the odd pothole in the shimmering black strip of road. Even the truck drivers drove responsibly.

It was almost a relief to leave the plantations and visit a typically disorganised tourist sight: the Athirappilly Falls.

The falls were not in my guidebook and it was only because I saw a group of Indian tourists walking up a path that I stopped. A sign warned the visitor that 126 people had been killed by the falls. Easy to see how.

In the West, the whole area around the cliff would have been cordoned off, while here, children and their school teachers stood right on the edge of the precipice – and even played in the deceptively calm pool of water just above the falls. As I foolishly followed their lead and crouched down to take a photograph, my sunglasses fell off and I watched them disappear over the side and into the river a long way below. Both the children and the teachers thought that very funny.

~~~~~~~~~~

In the port city of Cochin I visited the Jewish area. There's been a Jewish community in India since the first century, when the Jews of Palestine fled from the Romans after the destruction of the Second Temple. I don't know how big the community became, but it was now dwindling to nothing: most Indian Jews had emigrated to Israel, and the guide in the synagogue – a Hindu – told me there were only 18 Jews left in Cochin, the youngest of whom was a woman of 27.

I was disappointed to learn that the caste system had spread to Judaism and the two groups of Black Jews and White Jews seldom intermarried. Having said that, it's not as if Jews and Christians in the West don't have their own

divisions: Ashkanazis, Sephardis, Catholics, Protestants...
and various divisions within.

While I rode my bike in the town I got talking to an
Indian man riding an Enfield – as one does at level
crossings. When I mentioned a problem with my front
wheel suspension he led me to his mechanic, who'd
converted his front yard into a bike garage. His speciality
appeared to be customising Enfields; I've never seen so
many imitation Harleys, or so much chrome. A couple of
bikes had new names written in gory red paint, dripping as
if done in blood: 'Vampire' and 'Dracula'.

The mechanic was obviously very disapproving of my
scratched, dented and (I had to admit) extremely filthy
bike. His disgust increased when he learnt Big Thumper
was not even one year old. He pointed to the gleaming
Vampire and announced, 'This bike is nine years old.'
Nevertheless, despite his poor opinion of me as a bike
owner, his professionalism prevailed and he did a great job
on my suspension.

Continuing down south, I stopped for a couple of days
in the backwaters of Kerala – a long, narrow state
squeezed between the Arabian Sea and the mountains of
the Western Ghats. The land is fertile and criss-crossed by
rivers, canals and estuaries.

I took a river bus and rode my bike along paddy fields,
coconut groves and rubber plantations. Although
agricultural, the area is obviously wealthy: the roads are
well maintained and I saw numerous mansions and private
cars. This in a state that's been governed mainly by the
Communist Party since 1957.

It was tempting to stay longer, as I was enjoying the
tropical pace, but I was also eager to reach Cape Comorin
– the southern extremity of the Indian subcontinent where
three seas bump into each other: the Bay of Bengal, the
Arabian Sea and the Indian Ocean.

I wasn't disappointed. It really did feel like the end of
the earth. The beach tapered into a group of rocks
unmistakably further south than the rest of the coast.

There's only water between here and Antarctica, I thought, as I looked out to the sea. Nowhere else to go; the end of a journey – or in my case the half-way marker. In just under five months the bike had clocked 14,000km, from the Himalayas in the north to the tip of this triangle in the south.

But despite having seen so much of the country already, India still felt extremely foreign to me. There was so much about Indians I didn't understand. How could they combine great tolerance for other lifestyles which should theoretically offend their sense of propriety – witness their acceptance of enclaves of Westerners living 'alternative' lives there – with a capacity for extreme violence against other Indian communities, both inter-religious and inter-caste?

I hadn't actually seen any violence, and I found it hard to imagine the apparently even-tempered Indians raising their voices – let alone committing such atrocities that occurred at the time of partition with Pakistan, as well as the violence that still occurs today (such as the massacre of over 40 low-caste Indians in the state of Bihar in a dispute over land, which had taken place just a few weeks prior to my arrival in Cap Comorin).

Perhaps another example of this marriage of contradictions can be seen in the roads. I don't think I can exaggerate the mayhem in the streets: you see cows lying in the middle of a busy junction, overloaded and speeding trucks, swaying bullock-drawn carts, wobbly bicycles, gasoline-spewing auto-rickshaws, multi-passengered motorbikes, snail-paced tractors, cars driven by aspiring Formula One racers, dilapidated buses operated by stoned drivers – and, of course, hundreds of pedestrians who walk in the middle of the street.

The overriding rule, it seemed to me, is that *anything* is permitted – including driving on the wrong side of the road or going the wrong way up a one-way street – as long as you advertise your presence with your horn.

And yet all this noisy chaos is without malice: vehicles

cut each other off, overtake at the most dangerous places and pull out without looking; but tempers are never lost. I can't imagine road rage in India, and soon enough even I stopped getting irritated, because after all, traffic laws can't be broken if there are no traffic laws to begin with. Anything goes, as long as it doesn't result in an accident. (Supposedly, if there is an accident then tempers do fly; and it's not unknown for the driver perceived to have caused it to be lynched by an angry crowd.)

Another contradiction is the way in which corruption and crime live alongside utmost honesty. Every day the papers tell of thefts of huge proportions by politicians and top businessmen; and yet I could leave my motorcycle, loaded up with all my luggage, parked for a few hours as I went sightseeing. The bike alone was worth a multiple of the average Indian's annual salary, but all I needed to do was ask a shopkeeper to keep an eye on it and I knew no one would touch it.

Of course, I suspect *my* culture is just as incomprehensible to them.

Chapter 14
Steak au poivre in Tamil Nadu

I checked into a hotel on Cape Comorin and went off in search of a nice beach to spend the day on. As I rode towards a small resort 40km away with my bathing costume, towel and diary in my shoulder bag, I passed a roadside mechanic. I pulled over: my bike had been backfiring lately, and cleaning out the carburettor seemed like a good idea.

I soon regretted it.

Within ten minutes of leaving the makeshift garage I knew my bike was running even worse than before. I returned to the mechanic.

'The bike doesn't feel right at all,' I complained. 'It's jerking and stalling constantly.'

The man looked at me blankly: he didn't understand.

I sat on the bike and mimed it. 'Look, Enfield goes putt, putt, putt, then stops. And also the ride is not smooth at all.' I made jerking movements, but still he didn't understand.

'Does anybody speak English?' I asked the assembled group of a dozen spectators. They laughed and shuffled self-consciously in their flip-flops.

'Angrezi?' I repeated my request, this time in Hindi.

The group of men parted to let in the owner of the electrical shop next door.

'You are having a problem, madam?' he asked as he shook my hand. 'I will be happy to help you.'

I thanked him and said, 'Could you tell the mechanic that my bike is not working properly. It's jerking and stalling. I don't know what he did but it made the bike worse than before.'

The mechanic, upon being told this, shrugged his shoulders and sighed as he mounted the bike to take it for a test ride. When he returned, he announced that it only needed some additional tuning, and with great show he revved the bike as he adjusted the flow of petrol to the engine.

It didn't make any difference; I asked that he continue looking for the problem.

He muttered something and played with the screw controlling the flow of air to the engine, but still the bike sounded all wrong.

I could feel the mechanic getting more and more defensive as I was getting more and more annoyed. What on *earth* had he done to my bike? Cleaning a carburettor is supposed to be very simple – though still too complicated for me – so how had he managed to make it run so badly?

He tried tuning it some more, but when it became obvious he was failing he announced via the shopkeeper that the problem had nothing to do with him. In his view, some mechanical part was malfunctioning and the best thing to do was to ride to the nearest Enfield dealer in Trivandrum. In other words, 'Piss off, lady.'

It took me six very stressful hours to cover the 60km to Trivandrum.

The bike kept stalling, and it would sometimes take me ten minutes of kick-starting in the heat of the afternoon to get it going again. Finally, after it had stalled and I couldn't start it up at all, I sat dejected on the side of the road. It was six o'clock, dusk was falling and Trivandrum was still 15km away. There were no hotels in sight; I was going to have to lock the bike up, find a ride to Trivandrum and come back tomorrow with somebody from the motorcycle garage.

As I gathered myself, a well-dressed man, who'd been observing me from across the road, walked up to me.

'You are having a problem?' he asked.

'My bike has broken down. Do you know a place where I could leave it for the night?' I asked.

'No, but I know a mechanic just 200 metres away. I'm going that way, I'll take you there.'

He placed his shiny black briefcase on the saddle and helped me push the bike to the garage.

'I am sorry I cannot stay with you,' he said as he bade me goodbye, 'but I have a business meeting to attend and I must leave you.' He picked up his briefcase and I watched him walk away, his shirt-back drenched in sweat.

The mechanic examined the bike and identified a dirty spark plug as the culprit. With a clean plug, the bike started up at the first attempt. What a relief. Then he took it for a test ride and discovered that the tank was empty. How could that be? I calculated I should've had another 5 litres left. It didn't make any sense.

Anyway, whatever the reason I still needed some petrol, so he sent his assistant on a scooter to the nearest petrol station to buy a litre. Finally, and much relieved, I left. I figured within a maximum of half an hour I should be in Trivandrum... but that was without allowing for breaking down again only three kilometres further down the road. Swearing, I pushed the bike to another mechanic (the ratio of mechanics to Indians is higher than that of pubs to Dubliners). And this mechanic also changed the spark plug and sent me on my way.

It was now completely dark, and I could feel the bike still wasn't not running well; it stalled a number of times but each time I managed to clean the spark plug and start it up again. Eventually, at 9pm, it stalled for the last time and no amount of spark plug cleaning – or even a new spark plug – could get it going again.

According to my city map there was a hotel only 300 metres away; but what the map didn't show was that it was 300 metres *uphill*. By the time I reached the hotel I was nearly in tears. Actually, I lie: I *was* in tears, and the muscles in my arms and shoulders were twitching involuntarily.

The next morning I walked to the Enfield dealer, who sent a mechanic over to my hotel. I watched with nervous anticipation as the young boy dressed in clean blue overalls examined my bike and chuckled. In less than 10 minutes he found the problems, all of which were embarrassingly obvious – that is, if you're remotely mechanically-minded: (a) the choke was permanently engaged, (b) fuel was leaking from the rubber tube that links the tank to the carburettor, (c) the rate of fuel coming out of the tank was mis-adjusted, and (d) the petrol I'd bought when I ran out the previous day was in fact kerosene (although I'd paid the price of petrol).

No wonder the bike wasn't running well. But the really infuriating part is that nothing major was wrong with it: my lack of knowledge had turned minor faults into what felt to me at the time like a major disaster – especially as I was pushing the bike up the hill in the dark.

~~~~~~~~~~

A few days later I made it to Kovallam – a beach that was described in my guidebook as beautiful. However, it proved a disappointment: lots of new and ugly hotels and restaurants had been built right up to the seafront, and the strip of beach crawled with hustlers. It was impossible to relax on the sand because every few minutes someone would approach me to sell sarongs, necklaces, shells or soft drinks.

Unfortunately, a shake of the head wasn't enough to indicate that I wasn't buying, and the trader would stand expectantly – and very close to me – in the hope that I'd realise I really *did* want to buy a drink – or, more likely, that I'd buy one just to get rid of him.

However, I found the perfect solution: eight kilometres to the south was a luxury hotel complex with a swimming pool and a private beach where traders were banned; and although a room there would cost $100 a night, for a small fee I was able to use the facilities. Even though I went to India to meet the people, there are times in all long journeys when people are precisely what you seek to avoid – especially those who are trying to sell you something.

I got into a conversation with one of the managers of

the hotel complex, who asked me why I was travelling on my own. Usually I'd answer that it was because I liked the freedom of making my own decisions and not feeling responsible for anyone else having a good time.

Although that was true, there was also more to it: a large part of the pleasure came from the aloneness of riding my bike. With my helmet on and my big leather jacket, I felt cocooned from the environment. Yes, I was in it, but I was also protected from it: nobody could approach me, talk to me. I was in their world but they couldn't get into mine. It allowed my mind to wander without interruption – unless, that is, a cow came galloping across my path.

Riding with someone else, I'd be preoccupied with where they were. Too far back? Too far in front? I couldn't lose myself inside my head.

I accept it was an indulgence; if I were to lounge on a sofa for hours on end, thinking sometimes-frivolous, sometimes-deep, sometimes-ridiculous, sometimes-outrageous and sometimes simply stupid thoughts, I could be criticised for being a dreamer and a time-waster. For some reason, the act of sitting on a moving motorbike is seen – by me at least – as a valid occupation. So maybe that was the real reason I travelled alone: I like to daydream.

Of course, I could also come up with some more worthy – and also true – reasons: alone, I become more observant, meet more people, do not immediately vocalise my opinions and therefore perhaps judge less and experience more.

~~~~~~~~~~

I headed inland to Kodaikanal – a hill station set up by American missionaries in the 1840s. I expected to really like Kodaikanal, not just because of the cool weather but also because of the mountain scenery. However, although the drops into the valley were very dramatic, I found the partially finished concrete buildings depressing. Also, the empty drink cartons, the candy wrappers, the old newspapers, and the empty cigarette packs that littered every 'scenic' viewpoint all irritated me. It seems churlish even to mention this, since I'd been faced with litter ever since my arrival in India, but for some reason it was more difficult to ignore here than elsewhere.

Another thing that annoyed me – and this says more about me than anything else – was the multitude of honeymoon couples. My hotel almost exclusively catered to them, and I found the coyness of the brides and the bravado of the grooms annoying. I knew I should've been more understanding: they wouldn't always behave that way – in many (most) cases they were only just getting to know each other, and behaving in a way they thought was attractive to the opposite sex.

Picture the scene: there's a young couple walking along a mountain track. The boy leaps off the track and jumps onto a boulder overlooking the valley, and strikes a pose. He says nothing but glances down to his hand which holds the camera, and I imagine he wishes his new wife had it so that she could take a picture of him. She's saying something in an agitated, pleading but also almost giggling tone. I suspect she's asking him to be careful and come down. She then switches to English and says, almost crying, 'I'm afraid.' He smiles, jumps off and puts his arm around her shoulder consolingly. Everybody's happy.

Okay, okay, I know, you think it's jealousy – people in love and all that. But when variations of this scene were repeated all around me I found it hard to get that warm feeling all over again.

Three days later and my mood hadn't improved.

In Trichy I got into an argument with an auto-rickshaw driver who was refusing to use his meter. It's almost standard practice for drivers to quote a flat – usually between double and triple – fare for Western tourists and then feign incomprehension when you ask them to switch on the meter, or claim it's broken. Although I accepted I'd pay more than the local rate, I also got very annoyed at that presumption.

I asked four different drivers to take me to the main fort in Trichy, and at the fourth attempt I launched into a long tirade about how he was giving Indian auto-rickshaw drivers a bad reputation. I think he gave me the Indian equivalent of 'get lost' – at the very least – and accelerated away. After such an outburst I was, of course, too proud to hire another rickshaw, and I walked the half-hour back to my hotel to pick up my bike.

Then, the next day, as I was checking into my hotel in Tanjore, I tried to convince the receptionist that there should've been a discount for single occupancy (there rarely was, but it didn't stop me from asking). He refused and I insisted to speak with the manager.

The older man concurred with his employee. 'I am sorry madam, the rooms are the same price for single occupancy as for double occupancy.'

'That's silly – most hotels give a discount for single people,' I lied.

'This is a government hotel and our prices are fixed.'

I'd already unloaded my bike, but I almost turned out of the reception hall to leave... when it occurred to me that we were arguing over a couple of dollars. Why cut my nose to spite my face again? Instead, with bad grace, I sighed and said, 'Okay, fine, I'll take the room.'

That evening I had dinner at one of the best restaurants in town, where I met a young Dutch couple who'd arrived in India only a week before. They'd been suffering from some sort of stomach problem ever since landing, and today was their first day more or less back to normal. Despite the bad start they were loving everything about their trip.

'We've always been interested by Eastern religions,' the girl said.

'People here understand that spiritual values are more important than material values,' her companion added.

'Yes,' the girl agreed. 'Even poor people seem to have

an inner peace we don't find back home.'

'Don't you find the begging difficult?' I asked.

'No,' she answered. 'It is our duty as rich tourists to pay these people for the wisdom they teach us.'

Christ! Were these people for real?

I concentrated on my dish of rice with a sauce of prawn and cashew nuts. But where were the cashew nuts? I called the waiter over.

'Excuse me, I ordered prawn and cashew nuts, but I can't find even a single cashew nut.'

He laughed, 'No cashew nuts? Ha, ha!' ...and walked away.

'What's so funny about that?' I mumbled to my companions.

I called him back. 'Could I speak to the manager, please?'

The manager, dressed in a suit and tie, came to our table.

'What seems to be the problem, madam?'

I explained.

'Ah, but you see, madam, we use cashew nut *powder* here, not whole cashew nuts.'

'Really? So how come I can't taste them?'

'Probably because of the spices; we use strong spices in India.'

'Is that so?' I said, sarcastically.

He shrugged.

After he'd left our table, I turned to the Dutch couple and realised they were squirming in embarrassment. I was behaving atrociously.

I remembered, months before, promising myself that I wouldn't turn into one of those sour-faced tourists who assumes everybody's out to cheat them. I suspect that Dutch couple thought it was already too late.

After lunch I set off on my bike to Calimere Bird Sanctuary on the Bay of Bengal, and it took a beautiful ride to put me back in a good mood.

Usually I'd do most of my riding in the morning and

try to reach my destination by early afternoon. That day, however, I left at three o'clock, thus missing the hottest part of the day, and rode alongside a brilliant and sparkling blue river with the sun behind me. At around five o'clock the country lanes filled up with farmers and schoolchildren going home at the end of their day. They were obviously glad to finish work/school and I got many waves and smiles.

I arrived at the bird sanctuary just before sunset and was allocated one of the ten empty rooms in the government forest lodge. Although I was the only guest, I had to promise the forest ranger I'd leave by 10am the next day, as a group of government officials and scientists were taking over the lodge. Preparations were in full swing for their arrival, with the staff putting up colourful paper banners to welcome them. This was obviously a big event and I could feel the excitement as they argued about where to place the banners.

I climbed onto the roof of the lodge and watched a fiery sunset, and although I could only see a few birds in the distance, silhouetted against the sky, I heard a cacophony as each bird species tried to outdo the others.

The next day I went into the reserve to see the birds, but it turned out hearing them at sunset was the closest I'd get to the local feathered wildlife. The marshes were the breeding grounds for many migratory birds – a board in the lodge listed 243 species – but most had already left for cooler climates, or perhaps simply hidden.

I then tried to get into another part of the sanctuary, where blackbucks lived, but the entrance gate was padlocked. That surprised me since the forest ranger himself had told me about this section of the sanctuary. I looked around and noticed, a few metres to the left of the gate, amongst the bushes, a gap in the fence just wide enough for my bike.

I squeezed Big Thumper through the gap and rode into open, flat fields. There were no paths – just a mesh of narrow tracks on a flat, featureless plain, and the odd bush.

I could see blackbucks on the horizon, but every time I tried to approach them the thumping noise of my bike chased them away. After an hour of riding I reached a large area of thorn bushes. Remembering what those thorns can do to tyres, I turned around. I found my way back to the gap in the fence by following my own wandering tracks.

Continuing the nature reserve theme, I rode 150km north towards Chidambaram to stay on an island set in a protected area of backwaters and mangrove forests. I parked my bike on the mainland and took a small rowing boat to the island, where a hotel rented five cottages and fishermen lived in a small village three kilometres away. I booked into one of the cottages and then tried to walk to the village, but again got lost and decided to turn back as my feet started sinking into the swampy mud.

As the other cottages were all empty, this felt like my private fiefdom and I had the full (but unobtrusive) attention of the guard, who came to check on me every couple of hours and would bring me back supplies from the shops whenever he went over to the mainland. I spent a couple of days reading, doing stretching exercises and writing in my diary.

Early one morning I hired the guard to take me in his rowing boat deeper into the mangrove forest and onto some of the more than 4,000 canals in the area. Although very impressive and apparently peaceful, the canals were the breeding grounds of the most ferocious army of mosquitoes I'd ever encountered. They managed to get me through my shirt, jeans and socks. Of course, they completely ignored the rower, who also informed me that there was malaria in the region – so I rushed back to my room to take the weekly malaria pills I should've taken two days before.

~~~~~~~~~~

On my way up the Bay of Bengal I stopped for lunch in

the town of Pondicherry, which used to be a French colony and today retains a strong French flavour in its architecture – and, more importantly to me, in its restaurants. I was served my first beef steak in India by a waiter who spoke fluent French. It was delicious.

Mahabalipuram (after constantly stopping for directions that name just rolls off the tongue – more or less) is a small, scenic town 60km south of Madras (now called Chennai). It's built along the sea front and is full of shops and stalls selling sculptures of Hindu deities carved out of soapstone and wood. Walking down the street, you can hear the tapping of the carvers' chisels behind the doorways.

Although a beautiful little town, it stinks – literally. I stayed in a lovely cottage just by the beach, and enjoyed sitting out in the courtyard under the shade of coconut palms and bougainvillea... until, that is, I noticed a smell of faeces mixed with the smell of the sea and the tropical flowers. The beach just outside the walls of the garden was the villagers' toilet, and the incense stick on the coffee table did little to help.

I pushed on to Chennai, which, despite being the fourth-largest city in India, has a small-town feel to it. This was in contrast to the numerous small towns I'd been through that felt like frantic, major industrial cities. Chennai has a very impressive marina, and the traffic is controlled by an extensive one-way system that's generally obeyed by road users.

While walking around the city I came across a large crowd of young people outside a cinema. They were waiting to buy tickets to see the film *Titanic*, and the queue went right around the building. As I walked past, a young man asked me if I could go to the Ladies Queue to buy twelve tickets for the film.

Most places, including cinemas, post offices and train stations, have a separate – and much shorter – line for women; and if there isn't a separate queue, women can simply walk up to the counter in front of all the men.

Pleased that he'd at least noticed I was a woman, I agreed.

The next day I loaded my bike onto a train to Mumbai – a journey of 30 hours. I was going back to Mumbai to catch a flight to Israel, where my sister was getting married. I'd be coming back to India a couple of weeks later.

This was my first train trip in India and I was quite excited about it. The rail network is the largest single employer in the world, and it's an incredibly complex but efficient transport system. Since it was such a long journey, I'd booked a first-class berth in a four-passenger compartment. Unfortunately, what I'd hoped would be a break turned out to be very unpleasant. Both the air-conditioning and the fan were broken, and I got food poisoning from an omelette I bought at one of the many stops during the journey. I spent the next 20 hours being violently sick.

I'm sure the train went through some very nice scenery, but what I'll remember of this journey were my numerous trips to the increasingly dirty toilet, and the suffocating heat.

When the train arrived in Mumbai, the railway staff unloaded my bike with the same level of care they used for the post-bags... and broke my clutch lever. I gingerly rode up to Malabar Hills to stay with an Indian family I'd been put in touch with by a friend in London. I'd be leaving my bike and most of my gear with them for the next two weeks while I was in Israel.

~~~~~~~~~~~

Israel felt like a modern Western country rather than the exotic oriental place I remembered. I had thought that Israeli drivers were the most undisciplined drivers in the world, but now they appeared as docile as sedated sheep. Even the food seemed rather plain and a bit tasteless.

I was glad to be seeing my family here rather than at home in London; this way I could pretend it wasn't an interruption to my journey but just a slight digression. And it'd be an opportunity to see whether people felt I'd changed.

Silly me. People spend a lot less time thinking about us than we assume. And family dynamics tend to stay pretty much constant. It seems we just go back to the role we had during childhood; I may feel pretty confident now, but I'm still intimidated by my father, still guilt-ridden by the worries I cause my parents, and still bossed around by my older siblings.

~~~~~~~~~~~~

When I returned to Mumbai and my bike, I had another long journey ahead of me. I was aiming for Calcutta, and had a choice between a one-week motorcycle ride in the pre-monsoon heat across the heartland of India, or a 36-hour journey in an air-conditioned train. I chose the train.

Chapter 15
Oh! Quel cul t'as!

I arrived at the railway station in Mumbai a couple hours before departure to check my bike onto the train. At the luggage office I filled in the necessary forms and had the bike wrapped in jute and cardboard for protection, hoping the 100-rupee note I slipped to the packer would help ensure he did an extra careful job. By the look and smell of the man, I suspected the tip would be spent on English wine, which is what people here call whisky.

Once all the preparations were finished, my boozy railway worker suggested I go over to my berth in the train, and half an hour before departure he'd come and fetch me so that I could witness my bike being loaded onto the train, as I'd insisted on doing. After buying five litres of mineral water and as many packets of plain biscuits (no omelettes this time), I installed myself in my carriage, chained my luggage to the bars below the seat and observed the goodbyes all around me.

It was now fifteen minutes before departure and the packer still hadn't shown up. I asked the older couple across from me to keep my seat and ran to the luggage car at the other end of the train. My bike was standing forlornly on the platform.

Breathless, I asked the porters milling around, 'Why is my bike not on the train? The train is leaving very soon.'

They looked at me, but no-one answered.

'You must load it now!' I cried. 'I have all the right papers, look.'

One of the men pointed to the inside of the luggage car at a Suzuki 100 and explained. 'Regulations say only one motorbike per car. Security reasons.'

My luggage was at the other end of the train, the train was pulling out in just a few minutes; I had to get my bike onto it. 'Well, can't you put it in another luggage car, then?'

'No, this is only car for motorbikes.'

Only a few months before I would've shouted, 'Why did you sell me this ticket if you already had another bike to transport?' Instead, I took a deep breath and went up to another employee dressed in a clean, starched blue uniform.

With my best smile, I said to him, 'Excuse me, I wonder if you can help me. This is my motorbike here and the porters say they can't put it on the train. What should I do? The train is leaving in a few minutes. My luggage is at the other end of the train. Should I go and get it off the train?'

He didn't answer, but walked over to his colleagues. They spoke for a minute. I didn't understand but I recognised the words 'lady' and 'foreigner'.

Whatever he said had an immediate effect: within a couple of minutes, the porters had unloaded the Suzuki and replaced it with my bike.

As I ran back along the platform to my car, the alcoholic porter – who had kept a low profile during the whole episode – ran up behind me, calling up to me, 'Madam, madam!'

I stopped and turned around.

'Bike on the train now. Everything okay.' He stretched his arm, his palm open. 'You give me baksheesh [tip].'

I did not. Instead, he got a very nasty look.

I barely had the time to run back to my seat before the train pulled out. Indian trains rarely arrive on time, but they always leave on time. I tried not to think about the owner of the Suzuki.

The journey, mercifully, was uneventful.

Many, many, hours later (40, actually), when the train eventually pulled into the station at Calcutta, our car was boarded by around 20 porters with bright red shirts, white lungis (a man's sarong) and turbans to balance the luggage on their head. The strongest ones got hired first, and at the end, only an old man who couldn't have weighed more than 100 pounds stayed with me. I had three heavy canvas bags full of clothes, books and motorbike tools I didn't know what to do with, as well as my helmet and leather jacket. The old man took my biggest bag first and placed in on his head; he bent over for the second one, which he slung over his shoulder, and he then reached for the third. It was only when I promised I'd pay him for carrying the three bags that he let me carry it.

We walked all the way to the other end of the train to get my bike. Although only 8am it was already over 35 degrees, so we sat in the shadow of the train along the platform and waited for the railway employees to open up the luggage cars. Eventually, one of the workers broke the wax seal off the car door, opened the padlock and tried to slide open the door. He heaved and pushed, but couldn't budge it more than a few inches. He called his colleagues, and between the three of them they painstakingly hauled the door open – and as they did so, boxes full of mangoes fell out. I looked into the luggage car: it was completely filled with mangoes, from floor to ceiling and from wall to wall. No sign of my bike. I looked to check it was the right luggage car. It was.

I asked the employees about my bike, but they didn't understand me. Resigned, I sat on my bags and watched them unload the boxes. Then, as they piled them onto the platform, I saw something sparkle. With relief I realised it was my left mirror. But where had the cardboard and jute protection gone?

As the unloading progressed, more of my bike emerged: first the right mirror, then part of the exhaust pipe, then the bottom of the back wheel... until Big Thumper stood all alone in the luggage compartment with bits of cardboard and jute scattered all around it.

One of the railway workers radioed the train driver to move the car down away from the mango boxes so there was enough room on the platform to unload my bike. Gently, they lowered the Enfield and I inspected it, expecting the worst. But apart from a bent leg frame, there was nothing at all wrong with Big Thumper. I loaded my bags onto the back of the bike and pushed it out of the station, accompanied by my now-despondent porter, who obviously feared his payment would be reduced by the easier return journey. I paid him the agreed rate outside the station and rode my bike to the nearest petrol station to fill up.

~~~~~~~~~~~

To get to the centre of Calcutta I had to cross the Howrah Bridge – known as the 'gateway to Calcutta' and one of the largest cantilever bridges in the world. It also holds the dubious distinction of being the busiest bridge in the world, with over two million people using it everyday. It must also be the most polluted.

Calcutta. It conjured so many pictures in my mind: the slums of Dominique Lapierre's *City of Joy;* Mother Teresa's Home for the Dying and the Destitute; the opulence of the British Raj.

But it was some days before I saw any of those things, as my first few days were filled with getting a visa for Nepal, buying gear for the mountains, pampering my motorcycle with a visit to the mechanic, and best of all, booking a five-day trip to Bhutan.

The only way to visit Bhutan, short of a personal invitation from someone who lives there, was to go on an organised trip; so I reluctantly agreed to leave my bike in the hotel's parking lot for the duration.

One bit of trivia I picked up: the musical *Oh! Calcutta!* has nothing to do with the city – it comes from the French *Oh! Quel cul t'as!* (Oh! What a bum you have!).

Because the previous couple of days had been national holidays, the traffic in Calcutta was lighter than usual – or so I was told. It still seemed pretty bad to me, and, added to the heavy circulation, I had the problem of getting to grips with a system of one-way streets. Almost half the roads are one-way, but which way depends on the time of the day and the direction of rush-hour traffic. I didn't realise this initially, and got very confused when I tried to return to my hotel after the direction of the traffic had been changed.

Since I was in Calcutta I felt I must visit Mother Teresa's Mission. At least, that's what I kept telling myself. I wasn't looking forward to seeing all that misery. So far I'd seen relatively few signs of abject poverty. (Actually, let me correct that: I'd seen no more misery than in Delhi or Mumbai.) But, of course, I'd only ventured out in the commercial and tourist centres of the town where there was the usual assortment of digit-less lepers, street urchins in torn rags and old men sleeping on the pavement – all begging more or less actively.

I was the victim of one such example of active begging: as I walked down the street a little girl of about eight attached herself to me. She grabbed the bottom of my t-shirt and pulled on it as she walked alongside, demanding money.

'*Baksheesh, baksheesh. Chapatis. Rupees.*'

As I had no intention of giving her anything, I suffered the amused looks of Calcuttan pedestrians for a few hundred metres. I tried losing the child by going into the first available shop – a travel agent – but she simply waited for me to come out before starting all over again.

I tried ignoring her, I tried refusing politely, I tried laughing it off and I tried getting angry. Nothing seemed to deter her. It was only when her persistent pulling on my t-shirt produced a loud rip in the material that she took off, running.

~~~~~~~~~~~

In preparation for the next few months in the Himalayas, I decided to fit a new back tyre to Big Thumper. It had already covered 17,000km and I was unlikely to find brand new replacements for some months.

The man at the tyre shop couldn't understand why I'd want to replace the tyre so soon.

'Madam, I don't want to cheat you. Your tyre is still in good condition. There is no need to replace it yet.'

'How many more kilometres do you think it's still good for?' I asked.

He took a good look and pronounced it good for 'another ten or twenty thousand kilometres.'

I may have been convinced if I hadn't been able to see all around me hundreds of examples of the literal meaning of threadbare tyres. So he fitted me another back tyre.

~~~~~~~~~~

On the outskirts of Calcutta there's a large park called the Botanical Gardens. It was founded in 1787 by a British officer of the East India Company, and is a haven from Calcutta's urban sprawl. I parked my bike by the entrance and walked down palm-fringed lanes, along glittering ponds and lush lawns shaded by giant trees. People were there on family outings; courting couples walked hand-in-hand, young girls played badminton in their saris and children swam naked in the ponds and tried to catch the dragonflies. There was no litter (despite an absence of rubbish bins), and no begging (despite the presence of a shanty town on the eastern wall of the park).

At one end of the park was a 240-year-old banyan tree with a canopy of over 400 metres – the largest in the world. A sign suggested there were 1,825 aerial roots from the tree down to the ground. Did someone count?

On the way back into town I stopped to visit the Victoria Memorial building and the famous bronze statue of a stocky, dour-faced, middle-aged Queen Victoria. It's probably a good thing the statue was erected posthumously, as I doubt she would've been amused by it. Inside the memorial is a quotation from Queen Victoria, carved into the wall. She said, of her Indian subjects in

1858: 'In their prosperity will be our strength, in their contentment our security and in their gratitude our best reward.'

I wonder if she actually believed that.

Eventually, I did go to Mother Teresa's Mission – known locally simply as 'Mother's Mission'. The building is on a major but not particularly run-down road in Calcutta. A door off a small alley-way brings you into a bare, white-walled room where the tomb of Mother Teresa lies; it too is white and plain. It stands waist-high, and carved in black letters is a quotation from the Bible that reads: 'Love each other as I have loved you.'

Next door is an office ('Mother's Office'), where a dozen foreigners were waiting to register as volunteers. They included two young Japanese women, a middle-aged Baptist man from Nebraska, a Swiss nurse, a young woman wearing a University of Ohio t-shirt, and a British thirty-something man who looked like he'd suffered from dysentery for at least a month (his trousers were threatening to fall off his hips and his glassy eyes roamed from object to object).

Without really planning to, I signed up to work as a volunteer for a week in a children's home in the slum city of Howrah.

A couple of days before starting work as a volunteer, I joined a group of Westerners on a visit to the Mission's leprosy home an hour north of Calcutta at Titagarh. While waiting for our bus, a young woman with a deformed leg and a speech impediment lurched towards me and grabbed my hand. She smiled and shrieked a question. It was only because I'd heard it hundreds of time before that I eventually understood she was asking where I came from. She then proceeded to ask for my good name.

I answered, and suddenly she shouted in my ears, while still holding my hand, 'Give me rupees!'

'No… no.' I replied with a hesitant smile.

She pulled my hand very hard and screamed, 'RUPEES!'

I tried to prize myself away but her grip was firm. Suddenly she let go of my hand, and with pure disgust in her eyes she said in a calm, clear voice, 'Fuck you'. Then, with both hands against my shoulders, she pushed me into the path of an incoming tram.

Time slowed to a crawl. I was sure I was going to be run over. I could see the driver looking at me in horror, but my legs wouldn't move.

Then, out of the corner of my eye, I saw a middle-aged man rushing towards me; he grabbed my arm and jerked me back just in time.

'Thank you, thank you.' I kept repeating.

I felt very shaken up – almost tearful. My first instinct was to go back to my hotel room and have a good cry, but the bus arrived before I could make my excuses to the Mission's organisers.

It was with a good deal of apprehension that I boarded the bus for the leprosy clinic. What would the people there be like? How would they see me – like the woman who pushed me had? A rich, selfish Westerner? I felt ashamed of going there. Am I just acting like a tourist who pays to see a bit of human misery because it makes her grateful for the life she has?

I was wrong. The residents were friendly, confident and proud of their work.

The leprosy centre houses 470 patients. It provides treatment as well as a place to live and work. I learned that because leprosy is a bacteria that attacks the nerves, sensation is lost in the extremities and the patient is therefore insensitive to burns or cuts. He or she then develops secondary infections that result in the loss of digits, or even whole limbs – often due to gangrene. If caught early, the nerve damage can be reversed, or at least halted.

Like tuberculosis, leprosy is transmitted through the air, but it only affects people who are already weakened. It's very difficult to catch if you're generally healthy. However, because of the way they look, sufferers are often ostracised from their community – or even from their own family.

If, after being treated, the patients are still unable to rejoin general society, they can stay at the centre to work. Many operate handlooms that make hospital bed sheets and the famous white muslin saris with the blue border, as worn by Mother Teresa's Sisters of Charity. Some make special sandals for leprosy victims: it would be difficult for them to wear the flip-flops favoured by most Indians, since many are missing toes. Others tend the vegetable plots.

We were introduced to a young man who'd been diagnosed at a very early stage and now had no visible signs of the illness. The centre, which is solely funded by donations, was paying for him to train as a truck driver. We also saw women rolling chapatis – quite a feat when you have no fingers left. The place was very clean, and once I got over the shock of seeing so many people with bits of their bodies missing it seemed a very peaceful and beautiful place, with a well-cared-for garden, flowers and even a fishpond.

~~~~~~~~~~

The orphanage where I did my volunteering was a two-storey house in a small, smelly alleyway with open sewers running through the middle, in a Muslim slum in the district of Howrah. The ground floor had a large room that served as the classroom, and above it were three more rooms: a washing area, a sleeping area, and a playing and eating area. The kitchen was outside on the roof under a corrugated sheet.

My work as a volunteer basically consisted of hugging toddlers. When I arrived at the children's home, the older girl orphans were bathing the younger ones; upon seeing me, half a dozen toddlers ran to me with their arms outstretched and demanded to be carried. I lifted a naked little boy who almost immediately fell asleep on my shoulder, while a little girl in torn clothes climbed up my leg and into my other arm. This set the tone for the rest of the week as the children crawled all over me, played with my watch, hair, rings, hugged me and feel asleep on me.

There were about twenty children in the orphanage, including two babies who looked just like those painful pictures you've seen during the African famines: oversized heads on minuscule bodies, spindly arms and legs, the wrinkled skin of a sixty-year-old and big, sorrowful eyes. The other children were well fed, although quite a few had skin rashes and hacking coughs. The sisters said it was tuberculosis.

I tried to play with the children but they weren't interested. All they wanted were hugs and kisses. I suppose they felt abandoned all over again when the volunteers left. One child especially stood out from the others for me: his name was Lobus and he was a very small two-year-old with a constant stream of snot running from his nostrils, a painful rash on his forehead, lower jaw and armpits, and tuberculosis. And yet, Lobus had the eyes of an optimist; they sparkled and laughed with you.

On my last day the older children asked to see pictures of my family. I was afraid that looking at other people's families would upset them, but instead they found my relatives hilarious. My father's dungarees and my sister's shorts got the biggest laughs.

~~~~~~~~~~

Since I was soon to venture back into the Himalayas, I decided to get Big Thumper into tip-top condition. In addition to getting a complete service and replacing the back tyre, I bought a tank bag so that I'd no longer have to fumble through all my gear to get to my water bottle and road map. I also had a fairing put up for protection against the wind and the monsoon coming in a couple months, and I even had the visor of my helmet polished to improve visibility.

It was nightfall by the time I finished all these errands,

and the streets were teeming with rush-hour traffic. Only one kilometre away from my hotel, and immobilised amongst cars, buses, trams and taxis, I saw a tram in front of me turn right and decided to follow behind it. I wasn't too sure where it was going, but at least we were moving in the general direction I wanted. For 100 metres I followed the tram, when I noticed in my mirror there were no vehicles behind me. Instead I could see a very large policeman, all dressed in white, sprinting up to me. He caught me by the shoulder, shouting that I'd gone up a No Entry road.

Even though he spoke in Bengali initially, I had no difficulty getting his point.

I took off my helmet in the hope I could use the 'innocent tourist' routine.

'Sorry, what's wrong?' I asked.

'No Entry sign, wrong way,' he replied, angrily.

'Oh, I'm sorry... I didn't realise. I was following the tram.'

'Show me your passport,' he ordered.

Shit. I'd left it in my hotel room.

He made me dismount and push my bike all the way back to the main turning, where a thin, dark policeman – seemingly his senior – was directing the traffic from an island in the middle of the junction.

The first policeman told me to wait by my bike while he walked over to his boss and explained the situation. The senior policeman then signalled for me to come over.

In a very terse voice he said, 'You went in No Entry road... That is a very serious offence. It is illegal.'

'I know, I'm sorry, I didn't see the...'

'Keep silence,' he interrupted. 'It is a serious offence, there is a big penalty. You must pay 1,000 rupees.'

Shocked, I replied, 'I'll have to go back to my hotel to get the money.'

There was a pause.

'Illegal. Serious offence,' he repeated.

I must've looked – as I felt – suitably contrite.

He came down from the traffic island. His face softened and he asked, 'Do you have anything sweet to smoke?'

A policeman asking me for hash? I didn't know what to say.

I smiled apologetically and said, 'No, I'm sorry.'

He also smiled, and pointed to a cigarette stand on the street corner.

'Classic cigarettes,' he said.

No need to tell me twice. I ran over and bought a couple of packets of Classics – one of the more expensive brands of Indian cigarettes – and gifted them to the policeman. This was the only bribe I ever paid in India.

I was later told by a Calcutta resident that traffic fines are 50 rupees.

~~~~~~~~~~

Leaving my bike behind, I flew into Bhutan on a 72-seater Druk Air flight. As we approached Paro, Bhutan's only airport, the plane banked steeply into the cloud cover and severe turbulence to emerge into a very narrow valley encased between high peaks. This flight is not for those who are scared of flying.

I smiled. *Bhutan. I'm in Bhutan.* The mysterious mountain kingdom.

Until 1974, tourists hadn't been allowed into the country – and even now their numbers were strictly limited. According, to the agent with whom I booked the trip, no more than five thousand tourists were allowed to visit the country in 1996.

In the airport lounge, before taking off from Calcutta, I'd met a young Bhutanese woman working for the United Nations. She was dressed in fashionable Western clothes and spoke perfect English. She explained that all Bhutanese schooling was in English – although not all children went to school.

She was obviously one of the few Bhutanese with a

university education: there'd been 44 students in her graduation class, out of a total population of 1.5 million. At least I *think* that was the population of Bhutan; the government seemed quite reluctant to give an exact number. Bhutanese government brochures published between 1979 right through to 1995 quoted a constant figure of 600,000. This UN employee quoted me a figure of 1 million, and my Bhutanese guide later told me 1.5 million. I tended towards the higher figure because of the many posters I saw in the country encouraging the population to use birth control.

I was doing this trip in much greater style than usual: a compulsory guide and driver picked me up at the airport and stayed with me until I flew back out. I got the feeling they weren't just there to make sure all my needs were answered but also to keep an eye on all my activities and conversations with locals.

Both my guide and my driver wore the national men's dress, which consisted of a heavy belted robe called a gho, knee-high socks, and big white cuffs at the wrists. The king of Bhutan had made the national dress compulsory in the towns, and failure to comply meant a fine of $4. According to my guide, Kinlay, Bhutanese people changed into Western clothes once they got home.

The women's national dress (a kira) was made out of a similar heavy cloth fashioned into a long dress and held together at the shoulders with round silver brooches. Most of the women had short hair, and until recently had been forbidden from growing their hair as only women of the royal family were permitted to have long hair.

Kinlay mentioned that there'd been some opposition to the rule on the national costume from Bhutanese of Nepalese descent, who made up approximately one quarter of the population. Most other Bhutanese were of Tibetan origins; they practiced Tibetan Buddhism and spoke Dzongka – a language very similar to Tibetan.

This was clearly a very religious society, with a monastery in virtually every village, however small. Most

Bhutanese families would send one of their sons to train as a monk.

I'd hoped to climb up to Paro Taktshang – Bhutan's famous monastery – but, tragically, it had burned down the week before I arrived. It had been reported that the fire was caused by the oil lamps being too close to the hanging tapestries. The caretaker monk had died in the fire. Kinlay had cried when he told me about it.

Instead, Kinlay and I hiked up to another monastery at the top of a mountain, where we had tea with one of the senior monks, known as the 'Master of Discipline'. The 38-year-old monk was dressed in a maroon robe and had closely cropped hair. He explained that he'd joined the order at the age of 11 and had been very happy to do so because he had little enthusiasm for his two other options: school or farming.

~~~~~~~~~~

It'd be an understatement to say that Bhutan is a very mountainous country. Everywhere I looked, my line of sight bumped into the side of a mountain. So much so that it was difficult to gain a sense of the ranges, their height or their distance. In fact I felt hemmed in, shut off from the normal world. Bhutan felt like a forgotten corner of the earth. The fact that television was banned, and that there was only one weekly government-owned newspaper, no doubt contributed further to this sense of isolation.

If one could not see that this was a real, living society, it'd seem almost Walt Disney-ish; a representation of what a successful tourist attraction should be like: smiling faces, natural beauty, traditional architecture, picturesque fashions and no pollution.

On the flight back to Calcutta there was a Bhutanese soldier who'd been wounded in military training. Apart from rudimentary first-aid stations and a handful of Tibetan medicine clinics, there were no medical facilities in the country.

Once reunited with my motorbike, I rode up to the eastern Himalayas of Darjerling and the state of Sikkim. It felt so good to be back on the bike. It was running well and the mountains were stupendous.

~~~~~~~~~~

I was lying on my bed feeling very sorry for – and angry with – myself. *How could I be so stupid?*

That afternoon I'd lost my money-belt with my passport, ALL my cash, travellers cheques, credit card and driving licence; it was so banal, and yet it was a crisis. I had no papers, and no money to pay for my hotel bill or the petrol to get back to Calcutta. There were no banks here that would do wire transfers.

I didn't know whether my money belt was lost or stolen. It usually resided in the inside pocket of my leather jacket; perhaps I'd missed the pocket and it had slipped out? The seven hours since discovering the loss had been spent at the police station and wandering the streets of Gangtok in Sikkim in the dark, and in torrential rain, with a flashlight, hoping I'd find it lying in some gutter.

I tried to convince myself that someone would find it and turn it in at the police station the next day. It might be soggy, the cash may be missing, but the most important things would be there.

I wished the rain would stop; I had visions of my passport turning to pulp.

~~~~~~~~~~

I woke up the next morning cheered by a dream in which I'd found my money-belt. The sun was shining and I set off again to explore all the places I could've dropped it: the Buddhist monastery, the park, the restaurant and the chemist. Three times I did the circuit and three times I went back to the police station. But eventually, at noon, I had to give up and I went back to the police station to appeal to the top man for a permit allowing me to leave this Indian state, as I was in a border area that required special permission from the police.

Not only did he issue a letter to show at the checkpoint, but he also lent me money out of his own pocket to settle my hotel bill and to get me back to Calcutta, which was two days' riding away. This also allowed me to buy my first meal since lunch the previous day.

Lessons to be learnt: *wear* the money-belt and hide some cash in your luggage. Fortunately, I had the numbers of my lost travellers cheques, a photocopy of my passport, the number of my entry visa and an impression of my credit card.

(Two months later a young English traveller found my papers, minus the travellers cheques and the cash, in a cabin in the mountains of Nepal. He returned it to the British Embassy in Kathmandu.)

A few days later I was back in Calcutta, where I replaced my passport, credit card and travellers cheques in only two days. Whoever said India was inefficient? The only problem was getting a new Indian visa in my passport: I could either wait two weeks while they checked that I had indeed entered the country where and when I said I had, or I could get a stamp allowing me to cross into Nepal within the next seven days, where I could apply for a new Indian visa. I chose the latter.

However, mentally, I wasn't back to normal. I could've kicked myself for being so stupid; it had been such a basic mistake to make. You'd think that after eight months on the road I would've had the sense to be a bit more careful with my money-belt. In addition, I now started to think of all the other things that could go wrong – especially the possibility of having an accident. And yet, that thought didn't make me any more careful. If anything I was riding more recklessly than before, and certainly much too fast.

I'd rushed down Highway 34 back to Calcutta, and

now I was rushing back up the same highway towards Nepal. There were hundred of trucks on the road and I seemed obsessed with overtaking each one of them. I knew I was going too fast: travelling like that for nine hours a day on the motorbike was simply not sustainable. Besides, I wasn't particularly enjoying it. The trees were in full bloom but I barely paid attention to the riot of oranges, yellows, whites, pinks and mauves. There were palaces and mosques to visit along the way, but I refused to get off the bike. I was angry with myself and angry with the world.

Chapter 16
Nepal

I left my last hotel in India early in the morning and had another long and gruelling day. I hated retracing my route, and I just wanted to get the money-belt episode behind me. What a relief when I got off Highway 34 and branched off towards Nepal.

It was as if my trip was starting again.

The border crossing at Panitanki looked deserted and I had to wake up the Indian official from his post-lunch nap; on the other side of the no-man's land his Nepali equivalent was also sleeping on a bench behind his desk.

I then had trouble finding the immigration hut, as the Nepali side of the border looked more like a building site than an international border crossing. There were piles of gravel, barrels of black smoking tar, antique bulldozers, load-carrying bullocks, and frighteningly young-looking boys and girls preparing the road surface for the bitumen. I got off my bike and wandered around the site asking for the border official, but none of the young workers understood me.

Eventually I gave up and got back on my bike, thinking the immigration building must be further on. Just as I was pulling out, a soldier ran out of a dilapidated hut. He didn't speak English but made it very clear to me – mainly by waving his over-the-shoulder gun – that I should get off my bike and go into a small shelter partially hidden by a large, ruminating cow.

Once all the papers were stamped and signed, I started the journey towards Kathmandu.

What a thrill: newly sealed road, no potholes, three lanes… and best of all, no trucks. Not since Rajasthan, five months ago, had I experienced such a great road. Big Thumper seemed just as impressed, and decided to show off by hitting its maximum speed of 120km per hour.

Surprisingly, this road was straight and flat and not even 200 metres above sea level. The Himalayas were somewhere far to my right, only faintly discernible through the afternoon haze.

After a couple of hours I turned towards the mountains, but soon this wonderful tarmacked road deteriorated and eventually became a steep and rocky trail (when it wasn't a ribbon of slimy brown mud). I found the effort of steering the bike painful, not only on my arms and shoulders but also in my lower back. Eventually I discovered that it was much more comfortable to sit as far back on the seat as possible and let the back wheel absorb most of the shock. I later learned that this constitutes Lesson One of any trail bike riding course. In my case it took over eight months of riding to learn this. (A sports bra would also have helped.)

The next day, after retracing my route back to the main road in the plains, I continued in the direction of Kathmandu and stayed in a small mountain village called Daman, where eight out of the world's ten highest peaks are visible, including Everest and Annapurna – or so they say. When I arrived I could see only clouds.

In the morning I woke up to rain and resigned myself to a day of drinking butter tea – which to me tastes even worse than Indian tea – and tinkering with my bike. By tinkering I mean tightening all the nuts and bolts, checking the oil and running a cloth over the tank and the mud guards. However, just as the day ended, the daughter of the guesthouse owner called for me.

'The mountains are visible. Come and see.'

I ran up to the top of an ugly observation tower to watch the High Himalayas come out of the milky white sky. It remains one of the most moving sights I have ever seen. Each mountain emerged like a shy child actress being coaxed on stage by an anxious mother. Reluctantly they appeared on the stage, one by one, until the cast was complete and it filled not just the horizon but most of the sky too. And as the sun set, the peaks changed from a pale milky blue to a warm pink, and at last to a fiery orange.

I saw my first and only glimpse of Mount Everest. From this vantage point it looked like only a minor peak, overshadowed by its more dramatic sisters of Annapurna South, Fishtail and Dhaulagiri.

As I left Daman the next morning along another difficult mountain road, I passed a small village with a puncture repair shop where I stopped to check the air pressure in my tyres. I suspected it might be getting a bit low since the steering still felt very heavy. The man who checked it burst out laughing: the pressure was indeed ridiculously low. Rather than the usual 30psi it was only 10psi. No surprise, then, that I'd been finding the riding a bit tough on my arms. In comparison, the rest of the journey to Kathmandu felt effortless – even when the traffic built up around the capital.

In Kathmandu, Buddhists were celebrating the anniversary of the birth of the Buddha by throwing a big party in the capital's main temple (Swayanbhunath). There was nothing solemn about the occasion: inside the temple complex vendors sold ice cream, soft drinks and beer, and big pots of cooked food were placed on the ground next to statues of deities. Initially I assumed the food was a religious offering, until I saw a whole family sit down on the ground and eat off banana leaves.

Everybody seemed in a joyful mood, enjoying a pleasant afternoon out with family.

Ironically, it was on this day (May 11, 1998) – the anniversary of the birth of one of the most peace-loving historical figures – that the Indian government controversially detonated its first nuclear test bombs since 1974.

~~~~~~~~~~

I was nearing the end of a six-day trek through the Himalayas north of Kathmandu, with only three hours of walking to go before I reached the village of Syabru Bensi, where my bike was waiting to take me back to the capital.

The sun was shining through the canopy and I was sitting at a table outside my guesthouse with the Langtang River thundering below in the narrow gorge. It was only nine o'clock in the morning and I wanted to stay for a few more hours rather than rush back to the road with its trucks and buses.

However, there were two Nepali soldiers sitting at a nearby table and one of them was already severely drunk. He tried to have a conversation with me, but never got beyond the 'Where are you going?' and 'Where are you from?' When I answered he nodded knowingly and stumbled off into the little shop that sold everything from chocolate, socks, and – of more interest to him – rakshi (a cheap alcohol made out of distilled millet). He reappeared a few minutes later and repeated his two questions.

There were many soldiers in this valley because we were only a few kilometres, as the crow flies, from the border with Tibet. Of course, getting to Tibet is not a simple affair, since the paths there cross mountains over 6,000 metres high. This is the route many Tibetan refugees take, carrying whatever possessions they can manage on their backs.

I loved the trekking. It was quite steep on some stretches but manageable, and I seldom walked more than six hours a day. I decided if I came back to Nepal to do a longer trek I'd come after the rainy season when the views are crystal-clear. Still, even though it rained a couple of times, the scenery was stunning.

The most difficult part of the trek had been riding the bike to the start of it: an eight-hour journey that covered only 120km, on an extremely bumpy road. But the bus ride would have been worse: I saw a tourist emerge out of the bus with a cut lip and a bruised shin.

For a little while I'd ridden behind the bus and seen it lurch worryingly from side to side. It had been full, with an additional twenty people sat on the roof holding on very tightly. I was told that every year people fall off the roofs of buses and into the ravines below.

I'd passed an army checkpoint where I was asked to produce my driving licence, which I'd lost along with my money-belt. In all those months, not once had I been asked to show my licence – until now. I feigned incomprehension and showed the soldier one piece of documentation after another: customs papers, registration papers, insurance papers, trekking permit, WHO card, and even a copy of my credit card. When we got to my family pictures, he let me through.

For the duration of the trek, my bike was stored inside an empty house in the village of Syabru Bensi. When I returned, I found the front tyre flat and no puncture repair shop in the village. Not surprising, since this mountain road was a dead-end and none of the villagers owned a vehicle.

Fortunately, on the journey up I'd noticed an enormous building site on the side of the mountain, just at the entrance to the village. It turned out to be a power station under Chinese construction. I pushed Big Thumper down the road and introduced myself to the Chinese foreman. He didn't speak English but we managed to communicate through sign language.

He agreed to have one of his workers repair my wheel but explained that it would have to wait until the end of the working day, and in the meanwhile he'd be happy to give me a guided tour of the power station. He ordered two older men to accompany us; one spoke Cantonese (or maybe Mandarin?) and the other English.

We walked 200 metres down a damp tunnel through inches of slimy mud and into a large, hot and steamy room as big as the inside of a cathedral. Since I knew nothing about the technicalities of a hydroelectric plant, and the translation from Chinese to Nepali to English was patchy at best, all I could deduce was that they were aiming to divert the river into the tunnel and into the large vault, where a turbine would turn the power of the river into electricity. This was the largest hydro project in all of Nepal, and a Chinese company had won the tender. Most of the workers were Nepali, but the top management consisted of four Chinese – two of whom, when I met them, were obviously drunk on the job. To give them credit, however, they worked until at least 8pm when I left, and when I rode past in the morning at 6am they were back on the job, none the worse for wear.

That evening, back in the village of Syabru Bensi, I had a silent companion: a young Tibetan boy, apparently with learning disabilities, who lived in the village. He seemed very interested in my bike and stared at it intently. One of the villagers explained that he'd been abandoned by his parents over twenty years previously; and yet he looked no bigger than a ten-year-old. He slept out in the only street of the village, spent his days wandering along that street and never spoke.

For entertainment, the villagers liked to 'make fun of the dumb one' (their words). In one game, a dozen surrounded the boy and threw small rocks at him. Every time a rock hit him, the boy turned around to look for the source. You'd almost think he was puzzled, except his face revealed nothing. The villagers laughed and another threw a rock.

Another game was to make a military salute, which the boy aped – and he even added a few marching steps to the mirth of the villagers. Although these games seemed rather cruel, the villagers did look after the boy by giving him part of their meals, and they also cut his hair regularly. In the morning, I observed a woman call him over to the front door of her house to wash his snot-covered face.

For the return journey to Kathmandu, I took a young sick Canadian woman on the back of my bike. She had a high temperature and was covered in hives – apparently from an allergic reaction. She'd fallen sick at the top of the trek, and the high altitude (4,300m) most likely hadn't helped. Ill, she'd walked for two days back to this village, and rather than have her wait another day for the bus, I took her on my bike and deposited her at a clinic in Kathmandu.

~~~~~~~~~~

I wasn't sure where to go next: maybe a bike trip to Jiri (which is at the beginning of the trek to Everest), or white-water rafting, or lazing around Pokhara's lake...? So many options, but none excited me. Was I reaching that blasé attitude of the travel-weary? If so, I thought, maybe I should head home. Or was it just physical tiredness from the trek and the long bike ride back to Kathmandu?

In just the one week I'd been away from the capital, a lot of the tourists had left. It was hot, humid and almost the beginning of the monsoon. Maybe that was why I was thinking of going home: because everyone else was. But it seemed such a shame: when was I likely to be here again?

What about going to Ladakh – that mysterious 'Little Tibet' my Australian friends Jess and Greg had told me about? No question of going back now; a few days' rest, a log into my e-mail account to read messages from friends and family, and I'd recover my enthusiasm.

As part of my enthusiasm-regaining campaign, I decided to stay a bit longer in Kathmandu and enjoy the company of two friends I'd met during my week's trekking. Jack and Cora were an Australian couple on a round-the-world tour. Yes, more Australians; it seemed every other tourist here was either Israeli or Australian.

We walked around the streets of Kathmandu, marvelling at the incongruity of Western culture in this location: bars blaring rave music, young girls sporting mini-skirts and shop fronts advertising internet cafés. Of course, you also had the alternative medicine clinics, the second-hand copies of *The Celestine Prophecy*, the ethnic bedspreads and the hash.

Everywhere we walked in Thamel – the hotel district of Kathmandu – we'd get approached by young Nepali men trying to sell us dope. It got rather boring just saying 'no thank you' all the time, so we tried to vary our response.

'Hash? You buy hash?' a skinny teenager whispered to Jack.

Jack, long-haired and bearded, stopped, turned to the young boy and answered in his deepest and richest American Deep South accent, 'Don't y'all know it's a sin to peddle drugs? Ah Lord Jey-sus has said so.'

Jack leaned over and placed his index finger on the youth's chest.

'Y'all burn in hell unless you repehnt, mah son.'

That was a very quick and effective way of getting rid of persistent drug pushers.

One evening, after a night on the town with my friends, I took a bicycle rickshaw back to my hotel. At eleven o'clock, only a few late-night revellers were still out in the darkened streets of Kathmandu. As most of the journey was downhill, the rickshaw driver free-wheeled over the potholes and around the little piles of vegetable peelings. It had been a very hot and close day, and the damp breeze felt good on my face. We rode through Durbari Square with its intricately carved temples, now empty of persistent tourist guides.

Kathmandu was nothing like what its exotic name had conjured up for me: no winding roads, glorious views of the mountains, time-warped hippies or enlightened monks – at least that I could see. Rather, it was a polluted urban sprawl with nevertheless a charm, best felt late at night on moonlit deserted streets (and with a couple of mango daquiris onboard).

Having spent a few hedonistic days shopping for books, eating and having late nights in Kathmandu with Jack and Cora, it was time to leave. As I was stuffing my bags – 'packing' would be too kind a word – I felt the usual excitement at the prospect of getting back on the road, but also an extra dose of apprehension. I'd been thinking a lot about accidents recently. My riding was no more reckless than before; if anything it was better, and

Nepalis are more orderly drivers than Indians are. Perhaps my fear was due to the knowledge that within a couple months my journey would be finished, so the big accident I'd been fearing since the beginning of the trip would have to occur soon, if it was going to happen.

The road from Kathmandu to Pokhara − a lakeside town nestled in the Himalayas − was quite bumpy on some stretches. After a particularly bad jolt, the power on the bike died, and no amount of kick-starting could get it going again. As a car overtook me I tried to look like I knew what I was doing (even a self-confessed bike ignoramus sometimes wants to look cool). Nonchalantly, I crouched in front of the engine and, lo and behold, I found the problem: the wire to the spark plug had come off. I just needed to stick it back on and off we went.

One kilometre further down the road, the power died again, but this time the wire was still in place. I dismounted and checked for dangling wires. Everything seemed in order. Suddenly I heard a car coming up behind me around the tight bend; I pressed on the horn to warn it of my presence. No response. *No response?!* In a moment of clarity I remembered the man who'd sold me the bike telling me this would mean the fuse had blown. Very helpful, but where was the bloody fuse? And anyway, I didn't have a spare one.

Another car passed; I waved it down and asked the occupants if they had a fuse. As I'd hoped they would, the five Indian tourists got out of the car and took over. They knew where the fuse was and they knew how to wire it up if there was no spare. Unfortunately, what I didn't know was that fuses blow out for a good reason − a reason that should not be ignored.

I thanked the Indians and set off again... and a few minutes later my bike exploded.

Yes, just like that, with a bang and lots of smoke.

I looked down at the source of all the black acrid smoke and saw that the wires below my tank were an oozing multi-coloured mess of melted plastic. This one obviously wasn't going to be a quick road-side repair. I dismounted and started pushing the bike towards a village, which according to my map was two kilometres away. What had felt like reasonably level terrain when I was riding the bike turned out to be very much uphill.

As I sweated, a man on a motorcycle overtook me.

He stopped and turned back. 'Hello. Where are you from?'

'England,' I panted.

'What is the problem?'

'I don't know. The wires are all melted. Look.'

'Yes, that is a problem.'

You're telling me.

'Do you know a mechanic?' I asked.

'No, but there is a village this way.'

'Thank you.'

'Bye.'

I continued to push.

A young boy, looking after a cow in a field, saw me and ran up to the road.

'Hello, where are you from?'

'England – and you?'

'Nepal,' he laughed.

He walked along the other side of the bike.

'Why are you walking?'

'Because my bike is broken.'

'Ah.'

One more kilometre to go.

A motorbike came towards me. I squinted through my sweat-blinded eyes: it was the motorcyclist from before – now with a passenger.

'I bring you a scooter mechanic from the village,' he said.

With relief and gratitude, I pulled over under a tree and put the bike on its centre stand.

My saviour deposited the mechanic and turned his bike around. 'You want me to stay here with you? He is a trustworthy man, but…'

'No, no. I'm fine. You've gone to a lot of trouble for me. You go.'

He hesitated. 'I would like to stay because you are a guest in my country, but my friend is waiting for me at home.'

'No, no, thank you. Now that I have a mechanic everything is fine. You've been very helpful.'

The man rode off and I recuperated in the shade while the mechanic had a look at my bike. He called me over.

'See, problem is the wire is touching the carburettor, fuse blows and then everything melts.'

'Yes, I see. Can you repair it?' I asked.

He didn't answer but stood up, looked at a small hut in a nearby field and started walking towards it. Nonplussed, I sat back down and waited. So much of travelling is waiting, often not knowing why. Ten minutes later the mechanic reappeared, accompanied by an old man who was dressed in a dirty shirt and lungi (sarong) and carrying an old-fashioned transistor radio.

'You buy electrical wires from this man,' my mechanic instructed me.

We agreed a price and the mechanic cut the lead off the radio and used the various wires to replace my melted ones, with no attempt at trying to match the colours. Then, without appearing to pay too much attention to what he was doing, he wrapped black masking tape around the various wires, including the bike's accelerator cable. When I pointed this out to him, he shrugged and said it would still work.

'Maybe so, but what if the accelerator cable breaks and I need to change it? I'll then have to cut off all the masking tape to get it out', I insisted.

Laughing, he shrugged his shoulders. Then, as if to humour me, he re-wrapped the masking tape.

~~~~~~~~~~~

After Kathmandu, Nepal's most popular tourist destination

is the lakeside city of Pokhara, where many of the trekking routes and rafting trips start. A large area around the lake consists almost exclusively of hotels, restaurants and souvenir shops; far too numerous for the relatively small number of tourists – although in the high season (autumn and early spring) it's apparently difficult to find a hotel room. During my May visit, however, it was a sleepy town, alongside a lake so still that the mountains and pre-monsoon clouds were inverted with mirror-like fidelity on the water's surface, and water buffaloes – as well as the local children – waded in to escape the torpor of the afternoon.

On my second day in Pokhara, on top of a hill overlooking the Himalayan range of the Annapurnas, I met John – a good-looking British cyclist who was touring the world. (Now *that's* adventure and stamina.)

Despite it being only eight o'clock in the morning, he was dripping with sweat and resting by the road. We'd both come early to get a view of the mountain range before the clouds built up. I asked him to take a picture of me in front of the famous Fishtail Mountain. We got talking, and spent the next few days swimming in Pokhara's lake and exploring the nearby valleys on my motorbike. John was recovering from a recent bout of typhoid, so he welcomed the chance to rest his legs and lungs. I found him a very easy person to spend time with: quiet, undemanding and generally very laid-back.

On one of our day trips into the surrounding mountains, embarrassingly, Big Thumper ran out of petrol. There were some houses down in the valley and I freewheeled for as long as I could towards them. Eventually I left John with the bike and walked over to ask someone if I could buy petrol. The man I spoke to didn't have any, but he directed me to another house where a youth with a motorcycle offered to siphon half a litre out of his tank. John didn't comment, but I can't imagine he was very impressed; especially since he'd asked me before we set off whether I had enough petrol for the journey.

(I didn't realise it at the time, but meeting John would completely change my life. Back in England we kept in touch and fell in love. We now live together with our two children.)

Chapter 17
Escaping the heatwave

Having exhausted my one-month visa in Nepal, I said my goodbyes to John and made my way back into India and to the town of Ayodhya – a focal point of Hindu-Muslim conflict in the country.

According to fundamentalist Hindus, Muslims committed sacrilege in Ayodhya by building a mosque in the fifteenth century on the site of the birthplace of Lord Rama – a major figure in Hinduism. In 1992, the more extreme elements in the Hindu movement stormed the mosque and destroyed it. This set off major rioting throughout India, with thousands killed.

Nothing had since been built in its place, and any potential solution was likely to inflame the hatred between the extremists: one side wanted the mosque rebuilt, the other wanted a temple dedicated to Lord Rama.

With my bike fully laden, I rode up as close as I could to the site before the police turned me back. They were very polite in doing so – although I'm not sure I deserved politeness, given the potential for violence there. What I did see of the disputed area was not very impressive: it looked like a wasteland of rubble, with a dozen sick-looking cows standing there as if in a daze.

~~~~~~~~~~

India was in the midst of its worst pre-monsoon heatwave on record. So far there had been over 2,400 people killed by it. Temperatures were regularly hitting 45 degrees celsius – and even 50 degrees on some days. Newspapers were full of advice on how to avoid heatstroke: work at night and sleep in the day, and if you must go out when the sun's out, keep a raw onion in your pocket. (I had no idea how that would work.)

The press in Lucknow were also reporting the panic that was overtaking the city in anticipation of June 7th: Doomsday. Various pundits were warning the population that on that day, the sun would come 200km closer to the earth and all sorts of horrible things would happen. Some religious leaders were talking about divine retribution, and many teaching institutions and shops announced they would remain closed for the day. In my opinion they should've remain closed until the onset of the monsoon later that month: I found it amazing anybody could work in such heat. I was full of admiration for the policemen directing traffic in the middle of the day, with only a black umbrella for protection from the sun. The heat was so intense that the tarmac was melting, and my poor bike slid all over the place as if I were riding on ice.

Even while travelling on the bike, the movement of air didn't cool me down. In fact, there comes a point – about 40 degrees celsius – when it's so hot that it's more comfortable to ride with your visor closed, otherwise it's like having a hair-dryer on its hottest setting blowing into your face, burning your eyes and throat. Another cooling technique I found useful was to wrap a wet cotton scarf around my neck. I never did try the onion in the pocket...

One day, as I checked into a hotel in Lucknow, I suddenly felt very dizzy and had to sit on the ground. The hotel receptionist, clearly used to this, brought me a pitcher of water which I drank in record time. It was quickly followed by two more pitchers.

In my room, I discovered that the prickly itch I'd felt all afternoon on my forearms and upper thighs was a heat rash. I decided I had to get out of the hot plains as soon as possible. This meant I'd miss out on the Hindu pilgrimage city of Varanasi (Benares) – probably the most famous Indian sight after the Taj Mahal – but I couldn't face the prospect of walking around in this heat in a crowded city.

Instead, I'd head for the hill stations as soon as the local Enfield dealer had changed the bike's chain and sprockets. I shouldn't really have needed to change them so soon on a nearly new bike, but once again my mechanical ineptitude – and laziness – were at fault. The tension on the chain should've been checked regularly and tightened as necessary: a slack chain leads to damaged sprockets.

~~~~~~~~~~~~

Midnight, and my key-chain thermometer told me that the temperature in my room had only dropped to 39 degrees celsius. I'd covered myself with a wet sheet and was watching the ceiling fan cut painstakingly through the heavy air. A few minutes before, when the electricity had died, I'd had a moment of panic and was about to drag my mattress onto the roof of the hotel when the fan started up again. I couldn't stay here for long.

Lucknow has a number of tourist sights, and I'd decided to attempt them in the cooler post-dawn hours between 5am and 8am. First I went to the old British Residency, where the Indian Mutiny of 1857 had started. The buildings where the British had been held still stand as they did at the end of the 109-day siege that killed over 2,000 of the 3,000 captives. Today the area is a peaceful and beautifully kept park where Indian children play cricket and hide-and-seek amongst the bullet-riddled and cannon-damaged ruins, while their parents go for their early-morning constitutionals.

I also visited a nearby mosque and meandered in the intricate labyrinth built above it. This building was an example of Keynesian economics: it was commissioned by the local ruler in 1784 to provide famine relief to the local population. Another building, a few hundred metres away, was also a famine relief project, originally built in 1837 by Mohammed Ali Shah as his future mausoleum. Its courtyard housed two small, dilapidated imitations of the Taj Mahal.

Doomsday came and went without any disasters, and

the following day I left Lucknow and the hot plains to reach the hill station of Pithoragarh. The first day on the road I covered a leisurely 130km, and the next day a gruelling 320km – most of which was on small mountains roads – made worse by an additional 60km when I again ran out of petrol and had to backtrack to fill up. Fortunately the road to the petrol station was mostly downhill, so I was able to switch off my engine and free-wheel most of the way.

Running out of petrol once was embarrassing, but twice in the space of one week was ridiculous. Convinced it couldn't possibly be my fault – by my calculations I had another 100km in the tank – I went to a bike garage and asked the mechanic to check for a leak. He checked various tubes, and blew into the tank, but found nothing untoward. However, he thought the engine didn't sound quite right and suggested it could simply be a problem with the tuning. He explained that adjusting the air and petrol mixture should give me an additional 5km to the litre, bringing it back to the usual 30km per litre. It turned out he was right.

As I continued up the mountains, I passed yet another road improvement project. If the Indian Railway is the largest single employer in the world, I would think the Indian Department of Roadworks must come in a close second.

I watched three men dig a trench with a single shovel: one man planted the shovel in the earth, and then the other two pulled it up with the help of two ropes tied to the wooden handle. I'm sure two men with a shovel each would have done a much more efficient job, although clearly it's much cheaper to hire extra labour than to buy another shovel.

I ended a twelve-hour day with a tumble into a small gully – actually a drainage trench – by the side of the road as I swerved unsuccessfully to avoid a yapping dog. The dog seemed to come out fine from the encounter, or at least well enough to run away shrieking, and I came out with only a few more bruises to add to the collection on my legs. (I still hadn't completely mastered the temperament of the bike's kick-start.)

Lifting the bike out of the 80-centimetre-deep trench took six men and a woman... and some encouragement from a gallery of 20 spectators.

Thirsty, slightly shaken, and again suffering from a heat rash, I went in search of a room for the night in Pithoragarh. Unfortunately, every hotel was full of people who, like me, were escaping from the heat of the plains. In addition, the town was hosting some military exams and there were many young students occupying hotel rooms.

Eventually, at the fifth hotel I enquired at, the manager asked one of the students in a single room if he would share with another boy in order to free the room up for me. I was very grateful, and must have shown it a little too readily, as the youth knocked at my door a few minutes later and asked, 'Do you like sex with me?'

That evening I watched an English-language music show on television, presented by an Indian pop star. This is how she closed the show:

'A few days ago our beloved Prime Minister, Atal Bihari Vajpayee, did a great thing: with the nuclear detonations he showed the world that India is a great nation, a nation for world peace, for love. So in honour of this I want to play Michael Jackson's *Heal the World*. Remember, all you people out there: love the world.'

We then saw a video of the song, with images of children pleading for a world with no war, hunger or poverty. I'd like to think this pop star had a highly developed sense of irony; I fear she didn't.

~~~~~~~~~~

Next I rode through Rishikesh, a town 440km away on the Ganges where Hindus go for pilgrimages and Westerners for meditation. The day following my arrival was the beginning of a ten-day course called Vipassana, which was very popular with Western tourists. I wondered whether I should go.

During my journey I'd already had three opportunities to go on this course (in Dharamsala, Gujarat, and Kathmandu), and each time, although tempted, I'd decided not to. What was I afraid of? Well, how about: not being allowed to talk for ten days, or even read; of being told when to wake, when to eat; of suffering the physical discomfort of sitting cross-legged for hours, unable to move, while trying – probably unsuccessfully – to learn to meditate. I decided again to give it a miss.

I had hoped to keep ahead of the monsoon and maybe even make it to Ladakh – which is in the rain shadow (i.e. protected from the rain clouds by the high mountains) – before getting caught up. The radio and the newspapers had said I was at least ten days ahead of the rains; but they'd got it wrong, because barely out of Rishikesh I was overtaken. Not that it made much difference, as I'd been getting wet even before. But at the time, everybody had called these heavy rains 'pre-monsoon showers'; whereas now, the meteorological office declared the official start of the monsoon.

I had expected some sort of deluge, but the onset of the monsoon lacked the drama it deserved, especially after the excruciating heatwave. Over a period of a few days the temperature began to fall, the sky became hazy at first and then overcast, intermittent drizzle fell and became increasingly heavy, and the breaks between each downpour narrowed. That's the monsoon.

Riding the bike involved navigating through small murky ponds, whose depths I often underestimated. I'd subsequently find myself ankle-deep in water. I read that local children would sometimes erect a small platform in the water, and one child would stand on it with the water just reaching the top of his feet. Passing motorists would use this child to estimate the depth of the water, and would confidently ride into the puddle and flood their engine because the level was in fact much higher than they'd thought. The children would then appear en masse to push the car out. For a fee, of course.

~~~~~~~~~~~

It took me a few days to ride the 370km from Rishikesh to Mandi to stay with my friends Minal and Vikram – the mother and son I'd met last November. Vikram, who was still only 26 years old, looked considerably older than the last time I'd seen him. He'd spent the past few months campaigning for the local MP, running his farm and planning his upcoming wedding which would have 4,000 guests.

Being a member of the local royal family, I got a sense of noblesse oblige in his attitude. Even his choice of bride was just so *right*: a cosmopolitan woman from a traditional Rajasthani royal family (the Indian royal circuit remained alive even in the late 20th century). Vikram chose to fulfil the role he was born into, and he saw no anachronism. Actually, that's unfair: he saw the incongruity, but he also believed it was his responsibility to propagate a long tradition – even if it meant a loss of personal freedom and the need to put on a façade. Thus, surely, is the burden of royal families the world over. Laughing, Vikram told me how he and his future wife had to arrange clandestine meetings in distant towns where nobody knew them.

For the previous few days my bike had been making strange throaty sounds. I took it to a mechanic, who diagnosed a problem with the crank shaft and proceeded to disassemble my bike. As it turned out, he would spend an entire day painstakingly stripping the engine, identify some play in the ball bearings, spend a further half-day visiting every bike shop in Mandi in search of suitable replacements, and then work *another* full day reassembling the engine. If I'd known I would've left him to it, but Vikram recommended I stay in the workshop to speed up the process.

I watched the mechanic – a Sikh man in his late

twenties – while he worked. Unlike most Sikhs, he didn't wear the turban, and his long black hair shone with health. Despite the nature of his work, the nail of his small left finger was an inch longer than the others.

His work pace was very slow but methodical; he arranged all his tools in a neat row on the floor beside him, and he carefully placed the various bits of engine according to function. No risk of confusing the nuts for the gear box with the nuts for the oil filter.

Despite my presence, he'd stop every 15 minutes to greet a friend, have a cigarette, comb his hair, drink a cup of tea, or even – and I found that most irritating – jump on his scooter and take off without a word or even a look in my direction. Sometimes he'd come back a few minutes later, sometimes a few hours later. I'd never know. My presence there seemed inconsequential and unacknowledged.

I occupied myself by reading, pretending to study his work on my motorcycle, or talking with the odd customer.

Three young men rode up on a Yamaha 100 for a service. They started with the usual questions and then moved on to more personal ones.

'Why aren't you married?' 'You have boyfriend?' 'You like Indian men?'

I established that one of the three men was married, so I tried to direct my conversation to him, asking him about his wife and children, thinking he'd be less flirtatious.

I asked him if his had been an arranged marriage. Proudly, he replied, 'No, it was a love match. I love my wife very much.'

It didn't stop him from asking me, once the service on the Yamaha had been completed, 'I come to your room tonight?'

Later on, as I was still sitting in the garage, the 13-year-old boy who lived next door came back from school. He was eager to practice his English with me and he invited me to his home for a meal. As with most Sikh boys, his long hair was held up on top of his head in a bun encased in a piece of material – in his case white cotton crochet. He lived with his parents above their electrical shop in a two-bedroomed apartment. One room was for his parents, and the other room was for guests. The boy slept in the living room.

We sat there – not on the velvet-covered three-piece suite, or even the boy's bed, but on the floor. The walls of the room were adorned with pictures of the ten Sikh gurus looking down on us with benevolent expressions. The boy's mother brought out a meal of rice, lentils and salad.

His mother didn't speak English and the boy acted as our interpreter.

'My mother saw you yesterday with your motorcycle. She says you are very courageous.'

Smiling, the woman took my right hand in both her hands and spoke.

The boy laughed. 'She is asking if she can come with you to the mountains. I can stay here and cook for my father.'

As if on cue, we heard heavy footsteps coming up the stairs. Before he even opened the door, the man's wife leapt up to go to the kitchen and fetch his plate.

For the rest of the meal she never uttered another word, while her men bombarded me with the usual questions.

Chapter 18
Stuck in Spiti

After working for three days on my bike, the mechanic finally declared it sound and I set off out of Mandi towards the Spiti region. I had already tried this trip the previous November, but had been forced to abandon it when the road became a river and the army ordered me to turn back. This time I was doing the journey with another biker – Ariel, a 20-year-old Israeli I'd met at my hotel in Rampur, a day's ride from Mandi.

Our partnership had an inauspicious beginning. On the first day we tried to take a shortcut through the mountains and ended up on a dead-end, mud-covered track. We slipped and slid on it for over two hours before realising our mistake. Ariel, who rode much faster than me, fell off three times. (Or rather, three times that I could see; judging by the amount of mud on his clothes I suspect there may have been a few more falls that I didn't see.)

Three hours later, Ariel ran out of petrol because he was only getting 10km to the litre against my 30km per litre. He attributed this to his bike being ten years older than mine, although I didn't think that was enough to explain why his 350cc should consume so much more than my 500cc. I thought – but didn't say – that his preference for doing almost all his riding in first and second gear, and his love of revving the engine, may have had something to do with it.

We siphoned some petrol out of Big Thumper's tank and rode to the nearest station... to discover it only sold diesel.

However, the attendant, noting our frustration, asked if this was an emergency.

'Yes – I only have half a litre left in my tank,' Ariel replied.

'Okay,' the attendant switched on the petrol pump marked Empty. 'I give you two litres so you can get to the next station.'

Our next misadventure occurred soon afterwards, as I exited a tight bend too quickly, almost collided with an oncoming scooter, and was rear-ended by Ariel who'd been riding close behind me. We all came out of it unscathed, although my bike was *even more* beaten up now, and in addition its tail light, right-side indicator and mirror were all broken.

We stayed in the beautiful village of Kalpa, and the next day, unfortunately, it started to rain. Ariel continued to fall at regular intervals. I tried suggesting that he should ride a bit more slowly, but dropped the subject when he replied, testily, 'I've been riding since I was 14 years old.'

Half an hour later, he rode into a village and straight into a shrieking pig. The pig seemed okay, but Ariel, having gone over the top of his bike, had apparently bruised a rib. I was starting to wonder whether travelling with Ariel was such a good idea: he seemed so accident-prone.

As it happened, the next mishap was mine: puncture number four. Although by now I had both a spare inner tube and an air pump, we decided that Ariel should take the offending wheel to the previous village where we'd seen a puncture repair shop.

It took him three hours to come back, and I spent the time sitting by the roadside, surrounded by our luggage and worrying about Ariel having another accident and falling over the side of the road and into the river Sutlej, which was thundering 500 metres below us. How would I tell his mother?

When he finally returned, his only explanation for the long absence was, 'It took me a long time to find someone.'

Ariel and I rode together for another two days, during which he continued to skid and fall regularly. We reached the village of Nako, almost right on the border with Tibet, at over 4,000 metres high.

My first night at such a high altitude was rather unpleasant, with severe headaches and nausea. In the morning I decided to move on to the next village lower down, hoping that Ariel would choose to stay behind in Nako.

Although there are certainly safety advantages to travelling in a pair, I was finding it difficult to keep up with Ariel's riding – or with his conversation, which seemed to revolve around all the manly things he'd learned while he was in the military, such as how to kill a man without making any noise or how to hot-wire a Land Rover.

Unfortunately, Ariel decided to accompany me, and it was only two days later that we split when his bike's front suspension collapsed – no doubt helped by his kamikaze riding. Defeated, he loaded his Enfield in an empty truck to go back the way we'd come.

I set off to Spiti's capital, Kaza, to wait for the Ladakh road to open up. Although it was the month of July, the winter snows were still obstructing the road. Nobody knew how long it would take for the road workers to clear it: some villagers said two days, others said two weeks.

Kaza is a small town alongside the Spiti river, surrounded by the Himalayan mountains. The scenery is majestic: intense blue skies, jagged snow-capped peaks over 6,000 metres high, scree-covered mountains in various shades of brown, purple, orange and metallic grey; and all under a sun that seemed so much closer here than anywhere else. Besides a few fields of barley and peas near the Spiti river, there's no greenery.

One of the hotels in the town housed a tour group of eleven burly German bikers on a three-week bike tour of the Indian Himalayas. I'd already met them the previous day as I waited for three hours behind a broken-down truck blocking the road. Actually, it wasn't so much blocking the road as blocking the small river running across the road; while trying to cross the water, the truck had broken its axle and no amount of pushing could budge it. Furthermore, the track was too narrow, and the drop off the side of the mountain too steep to attempt squeezing my bike by the side of the vehicle.

As the hours passed I was joined by other vehicles, including the group of German bikers. While we waited for a truck from the road department to arrive, the sun melted the snows higher up the mountain, the water level steadily rose and I worried that it would be too deep for me to cross. Finally, at 1pm, the truck was hauled out.

I found myself at the front of the convoy, just behind a large truck that was painfully inching its way up the narrow road towards the water crossing. Suddenly it stalled, and a man rushed out of the passenger seat, picked up the nearest large rock and lodged it behind the back wheel to prevent the truck rolling down the mountain and into me. The man gestured to me to get out of the way; I swerved around his truck and continued up to the stream, where I pulled over to wait for the other bikes. I wanted to see how the others would manage the crossing before attempting it myself.

However, after a few minutes it became apparent that nothing was likely to come up the road until the truck driver had restarted his vehicle. In the meantime, two road workers, standing knee-high in the river, were urging me to cross. 'Go, go! Before water gets too high.'

'No – I'll wait. I want to see other people cross it first.'

'No, you must go now!' they insisted.

Nervously, I revved up and slowly entered the fast-moving water. Halfway through, my front wheel hit a rock and I wobbled, stalled and dropped the bike onto its left side, thankfully a couple of metres from the 50-metre drop to the left. The two workers rushed up to me, helped me right the bike and pushed it across the river bed and onto the other side. I was soaked, trembling and somewhat exhilarated. I'd been the first to cross.

Big Thumper was unfazed by the whole experience,

and despite its fall in the water it started at the first kick-start. I rode up until I could see the German bikers still stuck behind the stalled truck and I waved at them. They waved back, shouting their congratulations. Fortunately, none of them had been able to see my fall. I stayed to watch them cross; none of them fell.

~~~~~~~~~~~~~~

Kibber, a few hours' ride from Kaza, is one of the highest villages in the area at 4,200 metres. The fifty or so two-storey houses are made of mud bricks, their flat roofs covered with twigs for burning. Every family has a small stone enclosure built against a wall of their house for livestock.

In the mornings, the villagers open up the enclosures and chase out the animals with small stones, wooden sticks and whistles. The animals make their way to the village square, from which they're herded out to the pastures. Actually, to call them pastures is a bit generous: they graze on steep, rocky slopes where only a few stunted plants manage to survive in the incessant wind and blinding sun.

One morning I went to watch the shepherds as they set off. One of them – a small child of nine or ten – banged on a tambourine, and a few minutes later the animals started to descend upon the village square. First a cow came trotting down, but upon finding the square deserted it turned back in disgust. (One of the children told me that was always the first animal to arrive and never liked it.) Soon after, two adult donkeys and a baby one ran down, braying at full volume. More so than the tambourine, this seemed the real signal for the beginning of the gathering.

The goats came down hesitantly from various side roads and grouped themselves amongst a pile of rocks on the left of the square. Now and then a few younger goats made quick forays into the herd of sheep on the other side, irritating them with mock charges.

In the middle, the donkeys took their morning dust

baths, throwing up big clouds of dirt and braying with pleasure, while the yaks and cows stood there among the bustle, almost still, facing the morning sun like late-night revellers the morning after.

By now, the square held more than two hundred animals, and the four shepherds – three children and one adult – herded them out of the village, across a small stream and up a dust path to their grazing area in the mountains. Two women with straw baskets on their backs followed the animals out of the village to collect their droppings for fuel.

As I walked back through the village, a child ran up to show me a handful of fossils of snail-like shells. It's hard to imagine that 500 million years ago, this whole area was under the sea.

After waiting two weeks in Kaza for the mountain road 70km ahead to open up, and getting all sorts of information – or misinformation – about how long it would take for the road repairs to be completed, I decided to ride on ahead as far as I could and appraise the situation for myself.

After two hours on a very bumpy track, I passed a Western hiker who told me he'd heard the road had just opened that day for light traffic including jeeps and motorcycles. Great! I could be in Ladakh in two days. An hour later I rode up to Kunzum Pass, where at 4,500 metres I had a good view of the glaciers oozing down the narrow valleys. There I met a group of seven Indian university students on a cycling holiday. At this point we were only 15km from the supposed blockage. They'd heard it would take another three to four days to clear: not as encouraging as the previous, news but still not too bad. I could occupy myself with trekking in the area until then.

I continued for another 10km to the settlement of Batal, and on the way there my bike suffered its fifth puncture of the trip. There was no question of waiting for help on this dead-end mountain track; it was finally time for me to deal with this problem on my own. Fortunately, the puncture was on the front wheel (which is much easier to take off than the back wheel), and in the space of an hour I managed to take off the wheel, extract the punctured inner tube, replace it with my new one, replace the wheel, reconnect the front brake and pump up the tyre.

I was *very* proud of myself.

However, now, of course, I no longer had a spare inner tube. I worried about that, but laughed when I remembered that for the first few months of my journey I neither had a spare inner tube nor thought anything of it. Ignorance is bliss...

In Batal, a one-stone-hut settlement, I met an Italian trekker who had just walked over from the other side.

'Is the road open for motorcycles?' I asked him.

'You must be joking,' he laughed. 'It won't be opened for at least another two weeks.'

'Are you sure?'

'There are fields of snow and ice over five metres high, and at least one landslide that's more than 100 metres wide. I met a road worker who told me one of the bulldozers is broken and that the other one is not working very well. He said it would take at least two more weeks.'

The owner of the small guesthouse – if one could call the four walls made of stacked stones and covered with plastic sheeting a guesthouse – nodded in agreement with the Italian.

Shit. For the sake of 30km of bad roads, I'd have to do a detour of 600km. I *hated* backtracking.

I slept inside the hut, on the floor with four others, and in the morning, not yet willing to admit defeat, I rode up the 5km on the rocky path to the first roadblock. I wanted to see the situation for myself. The road, squeezed between the Chandra river on its left and a steep mountain on its right, suddenly disappeared into a wall of snow. Although all the snow had already melted on the mountain itself, it had accumulated on the road to form a snowfield the exact width of the road, 50 metres long and over four metres high.

To clear it, the Indian roadworks department had at its disposal the one surviving bulldozer, half a dozen road workers and some dynamite. I watched two of the workers climb onto the snowfield, where they buried four sticks of dynamite. They lit the fuses and jumped off the snow to safety. A few seconds later I heard muffled explosions and the bulldozer advanced into the snow. With the ice and snow now loosened, the bulldozer was able to heave the heavy blocks into the fast-moving river below the road.

'How long do you think it'll take to open the road?' I asked one of the dynamiters.

'We're almost finished. Today we are finishing the snow and tomorrow the other bulldozer will work on the landslide. Two, three days and you get to Chattral.'

'Chattral? That's on the other side, no?'

'Yes.'

I felt my spirit lift again.

Later that day, two Swiss cyclists came through from Chattral and stated categorically that passage on a motorbike was impossible due to big fields of boulders and snow; even they'd had to unload their bicycles and carry them on their shoulders.

Should I turn back? Go back to Delhi? Attempt another route to Ladakh? I was changing my mind every hour.

I really wanted to reach Ladakh because I'd heard it was a magical place: more Tibetan than even Chinese-occupied Tibet is today, with a lunar-like landscape over 4,000 metres high, inhabited by Buddhists.

I finally decided to stay in Spiti until the road opened up. I knew the crossing would be difficult, but after nine months of riding I felt I should have the courage to attempt it. In the meantime, I'd ride back to Kaza to get the damaged inner tube repaired.

~~~~~~~~~~

The manager of my hotel in Kaza was a 25-year-old

Tibetan Buddhist monk named Samdup who'd taken leave of absence from his monastery to live in town for the summer tourist season and help his sister run the hotel. His Head Lama, however, insisted that during the day, when Samdup was not busy, he should fulfil his duties as a monk and perform prayer ceremonies for the people of the village.

One day, Samdup asked another monk to take his place and came for a day trip on the back of my bike. We rode to a village two hours away to visit Samdup's monastery, which he'd joined at the age of six and would return to when the tourist season was over.

For the journey, Samdup changed out of his civilian clothes into his monk's garb: a long maroon skirt and sleeveless top, over which he wore a bright yellow fleece jacket. He completed the outfit with the all-essential baseball cap no self-respecting monk can be seen without – justifiably, given the fierceness of the sun at that altitude.

The monastery consisted of a square-shaped mud-brick building constructed around a courtyard; the temple, at one end of the courtyard, contained many tapestries, golden statues of the Buddha, and cases of books of holy scriptures smuggled out of Tibet.

Samdup introduced me to the monks and I joined them for salted butter tea. They spoke among themselves, and the discussion, in the local language, became increasingly vigorous. I saw this as an opportunity to excuse myself, thus avoiding another cup of that tea, and took a walk into the apparently deserted village. (Samdup later explained that everyone was either working the fields of barley or herding the animals.)

I walked along the narrow alleyways until I came upon a tiny baby yak that couldn't have been more than one or two months old. It trotted up to me and rubbed itself against my legs. I crouched to pet it, and the smell of my leather jacket seemed to send it into a frenzy of affection as it tried to suckle the leather cuffs and even climb into my jacket. It followed me up the hill back to the monastery and tried to go through the entry gate. (It was still there when Samdup and I left an hour later.)

Back in the monk's room, the discussion had calmed down and Samdup looked very pleased. He explained, 'The day after tomorrow, the Head Lama is calling a big meeting here and he will announce the retirement of the current management. We think he will ask me and my friends to take responsibility for the running of the monastery. We are the oldest ones here, so he should ask us.'

'Would you like the job?'

'Yes, it is very important work, usually only given to older monks. But he has no one else to ask.'

'So you'll you take it?'

'We think we will say yes, but we want some changes first.'

'Like what?'

'At the moment we have some employees who are not monks and who report to the Head Lama. We want to change that. We want them to obey us and not the Head Lama, who is too busy anyway.'

'How will this change the way the monastery is managed?'

'We think that this way, decisions that would usually take weeks or months to be taken, because they have to go through the Head Lama, will be taken much more quickly. We are young and we want to change many things.'

'Do you think he'll agree?'

'Yes, because if we all demand this, he will have no choice.'

Revolution in the ranks…

I spent the next week visiting more monasteries, hunting fossils and further damaging Big Thumper's front suspensions on dirt tracks. The news about the road ahead was still not encouraging, with some people saying it could take another ten days before it opened up to traffic. A policeman I met in the vegetable market, however, convinced me to wait just a little bit longer.

He explained, 'Everybody is working very hard to clear the road before we get a visit from the state minister. He is coming in two days and we must open the road otherwise he will get angry. It is already one month late.'

Only half believing him, I set off the next day once again for the stone hut of Batal.

As I pulled up to the hut in the late afternoon, I recognised one of the road workers sitting in the sun.

'How is the road?' I asked as I dismounted.

With a big toothy smile, he answered, 'It is opened. We finished today.'

I got back on my bike. I'd go across now; it was still daylight and there were only 30km to the next settlement.

He stopped me: 'Better to cross tomorrow morning before the sun is hot. There is too much water on the road.'

I hesitated. I'd waited a whole month for the road to open up. What if there was another landslide tomorrow?

But I was tired, and the smell of cooking in the hut convinced me to wait until the morning.

Shoes off, a cup of tea in my hand, I watched the sun go down behind the mountains, and noticed some people walking down a path towards the hut. They were six young Indian men who'd just come from a hike up to a nearby lake. Windswept, tired and hungry, they sat down for biscuits and tea and introduced themselves. They too were travelling on motorbikes, and pointed to three scooters (which I hadn't noticed) against the wall of the hut.

I was surprised. 'You're travelling on *those*?'

They nodded.

'But they're scooters, and there are only three of them, and six of you!' I exclaimed. 'I can't believe this; I have enough trouble on my own on an Enfield 500 and you're managing with two people on little Bajaj scooters?!'

I was even more impressed when they finished their food, picked up their backpacks and announced that they'd attempt the crossing right there and then.

'You're mad! It's six o'clock in the evening; it's starting to get dark and it's already cold. Why don't you wait until tomorrow morning?'

'No, we want to get to the other side so that we can find a phone to call our families and tell them we are fine,' the tallest of them answered.

His long-haired friend added, 'I promised my mother I would call every evening and it's been two days now. She will be very worried.'

If I were her, I thought, I'd be a lot more anxious knowing the risks you're taking to make that call.

The young Indians took off, and the next morning I set off for my own attempt. The first 10km were hard but similar to other tracks I'd been on; the next 20 were the toughest I'd ever encountered. I promised myself that if I came across anything as difficult as this on the rest of this trip, I'd turn back. When it wasn't big rocks on the track, it'd be sand, or mud, or snow, or a deep and fast-moving river to cross. Around every bend there was an obstacle of some sort.

Early in the journey I passed a Dutch hiker sitting by the road, treating his blisters.

'Can I ride on the back of your bike?' he asked.

I hesitated. 'I don't mind trying, but I may have to ask you to get off if it's too difficult.'

He was over six feet tall and broad; but at least he was travelling very light with only a small backpack.

Despite my initial misgivings, I turned out to be very grateful for his presence: five times he helped me push my bike out of trouble – three times in rivers where I stalled, once in mud, and once in snow. I used my clutch so much that eventually it gave up on me. However, after letting the bike cool down and tightening the clutch cable, it came back to life.

The feeling of achievement when I reached the other side was almost as great as that first day on the bike back in October.

Much to the amusement of a group of Indian road workers, I got off Big Thumper, did a little victory dance around it, kissed its tank and hugged my Dutch hitchhiker.

A few days later I met the six Indians on their scooters. Their bikes were still working and they seemed in good form. How they managed this road in the dark I'll never understand.

At least they had the decency to agree that it'd been a difficult crossing.

Chapter 19
Ladakh

The rest of the road up towards Ladakh was a doddle in comparison, and I felt rather superior whenever I met other bikers who'd come up the easier road from Manali.

'You think this is difficult? Let me tell you about difficult...'

The road to Leh in Ladakh goes through a two-day stretch with no villages – only temporary settlements for shepherds during the summer grazing season, and tents for travellers to eat and sleep in. By September, the snows would be back and the road would close.

On the first night I slept in one of the big white tents in Sarchu, where I was the only tourist. Apparently that year's tourist season had been very bad – whether because of India's recent nuclear tests or because of the increased fighting in nearby Kashmir, I didn't know.

After dinner I sat with the owners of the tent: a middle-aged Tibetan refugee couple and their daughter, Dawa. In the winter, the parents moved south to Punjab where they sold knitwear on street stalls, while in the summer they managed this tent. Although both were illiterate, they'd managed to send their two children to college. Dawa was a second-year business student in Shimla, and her brother was an officer in the Indian army based in Leh.

I asked Dawa when she'd last seen her brother.

'Two years ago at his wedding,' she replied.

'Haven't you been to visit him in Leh? It's only two days from here.'

'No, the buses are too expensive.'

'You can come with me,' I offered, 'if you're not afraid of motorcycles.'

She laughed. 'I'll ask my parents.'

I expected them to refuse politely, but they agreed to entrust their daughter to a complete stranger. In the morning, Dawa's small shoulder bag was packed and we set off to the second-highest pass in the world at 5,360 metres.

The journey was uneventful (apart from a bulldozer reversing into my bike and ripping into my luggage). The scenery was as beautiful as I'd come to expect in the Himalayas, with snow-covered peaks, narrow gorges and wide-open prairies.

Dawa was so light I couldn't feel her on the back of my bike; I even had to check a few times that she was still there. We spent a night in another tent settlement where, although Dawa's English was very good, the conversation was rather stilted due to her shyness.

After dropping Dawa at the house of her brother in Leh, I stopped at the only petrol station for 300km to fill up the tank. Half a dozen bikes and cars were parked around the attendant, who was trying to revive the flow of petrol by shaking the nozzle and repeatedly pulling on the lever. I decided to return in the evening, and when I did so I found him looking even more despondent in the middle of even more vehicles.

Nobody could say when there'd be a delivery of petrol; an Australian riding an Enfield reported a rumour that the army had commandeered all available supplies for the war effort in nearby Kashmir.

I gave up waiting and decided to ride back to my hotel. However, as I started up my bike, the decompressor cable snapped. Fortunately, the other Enfield rider turned out to be leading a group of fifteen Australian bikers on a tour of the Indian Himalayas, and he had his own full-time mechanic as well as all the necessary spare parts. Not a bad place for me to break a cable; certainly better than if it had happened two days before when I'd been travelling through totally uninhabited terrain over 5,000 metres high.

The next day I rode with the Australian group up to what's advertised as the world's highest road (5,660 metres). Although the way up the mountain was very scenic, with numerous hairpin bends, the point of highest elevation looked like – and indeed was – an old army depot: a handful of ramshackle hangars; some broken-down jeeps; a few other vehicles that looked ready for the breaking yard but would go for another few tens of thousands of kilometres; dozens of battered and rusted empty fuel barrels; and tired-looking soldiers who hadn't seen hot water for weeks, looking at the tourists with a bored expression that barely changed even when the Australian bikers dropped their pants to moon for the cameras.

However, when a smart army jeep drove up filled with equally smart-looking Indian officers, the soldiers' blasé look suddenly disappeared and they jumped to their feet. An inspection? No – it turned out they too were tourists who wanted a picture on the world's highest road. With relief the soldiers returned to their seats and their bored contemplation.

I started a conversation with the visiting officers, who belonged to a regiment patrolling India's nearby borders with China and Pakistan.

I asked them about the recent fighting on the Line of Control with Pakistan, where the BBC had reported over 60 deaths in the previous few days.

The oldest and most decorated of the officers replied, with a big, reassuring smile: 'No, everything is peaceful. This is a very peaceful area.'

Another officer added, laughing, 'Yes, and our nuclear test was a peaceful test.'

I'd been half-thinking of riding through Kashmir again on my way back to Delhi, but the officer's joke convinced me this was definitely not a good idea. Especially since a lot of soldiers ride Enfield motorcycles in these mountains (and I'd often been given military salutes by local children as I rode by).

~~~~~~~~~~

To visit Tsomoriri Lake, a day's riding away from Leh, I teamed up with three other foreigners travelling on two motorbikes. The lake is at an altitude of 4,520m and is extremely isolated.

As we set off I felt some wobble in my steering, which I attributed to the bike being unevenly loaded with one 10-litre jerry can of petrol on one side and another of five litres on the other. However, two hours into the journey my riding companions also noticed some play in my back wheel. As soon as they pointed it out I knew why: when I'd had my puncture with Ariel, the Israeli, the previous month, we'd refitted the back wheel in the night and I'd forgot to put in a small ring of metal, called a spacer. Later I'd asked a mechanic for a replacement but he didn't have any. Anyway, he'd reassured me that it wasn't an important part and that I could continue riding. Since then I'd completely forgotten about it.

I considered turning back, but decided to push on: the play on the wheel was only a few millimetres, and one of my companions seemed to know quite a bit about bikes and carried a full set of spares – although not a spacer.

The next hour's riding was spent worrying about whether I'd made the right decision; I wasn't enjoying the ride and kept imagining that the wobble was getting worse. Then I had the following thought: if I'd been on my own I would've already turned back; it was only because of some sense of safety in numbers that I'd pushed on. In other words, I was relying on my companions to sort out any potential problem.

I pulled over, wished them a happy and safe journey, and headed back. By then the play in the wheel had further increased. I had another three hours of riding to the nearest mechanic, and although the mountain scenery was stunning, I saw very little of it since my attention was fully focused on keeping the bike upright. The wobble was definitely getting worse, and it felt like the back wheel would fall off at any moment. In true ostrich, head-in-the-sand fashion, I refused to stop and look at the damage.

It was with great relief I got to the mechanic in Leh, and although he didn't have a spacer, he managed to conjure one up by hammering out the inner ring of a ball bearing. He said it would get me back to Delhi.

I took this as my cue to return to Delhi. My poor Big Thumper seemed to be falling to bits – through my own fault, I knew – and I was afraid it wouldn't be able to make it.

On the first day out of Leh, I rode out early in the morning and after a few hours pulled over to answer a call of nature. As I crouched down, I saw my bike slowly topple over onto the road: the sandy ground hadn't been hard enough to support the side-stand.

I quickly pulled my trousers up and ran over to the bike. This was the second time this had happened to me (in the same circumstances) and I knew I had to get the bike back up before too much petrol and oil leaked out.

This time, however, the leaks were the least of my worries: the clutch lever was broken and I didn't have a spare one. The landscape was desolate and I could see for miles around: not a vehicle or any sign of life in sight.

By pulling on what was left of the clutch lever I could just about manage to change gears, so I decided to push on. As long as the terrain was reasonable I'd be able to manage; the problem was when I needed to release the clutch slowly while revving up to get the necessary acceleration to get over rocks, sandy patches or through streams. I was often forced to get off the bike and push it over the difficult sections.

It was exhausting and very slow progress. But suddenly I saw another Enfield coming towards me. What luck! The rider turned out to be leading a group of American and British bikers and had a van with mechanic and spares following behind. It took their mechanic 10 minutes to repair the bike, and it only cost me a few hundred rupees.

At this point, probably not for the first time, I realise a

lot of readers will be getting exasperated with me. 'Good grief,' you might be saying. 'This woman is irresponsible: she knows nothing about looking after a bike and doesn't even carry the necessary spares. She goes around blissfully unaware and relies on other people to sort her problems out.'

And you'd be absolutely correct. In my defence, all I can say is that I'm an eternal optimist who believes that a solution is never far away – even on the most remote roads. So even when my bike broke down, I always expected there'd be a way to bring it, and myself, back to safety. At the same time, I also knew I shouldn't do like the previous day when I'd caught myself expecting my companions to sort out my problems.

There's a difference between asking for people's help and relying on it. In other words, relying on yourself to find help is not the same as relying on others to help you. So yes, I still didn't know even the basics of motorcycle maintenance, but I was willing to spend the extra time and money to find someone else who did. The challenge for me had become not so much one of learning how to repair Big Thumper, but of learning how to get it repaired; being independent doesn't necessarily mean being self-sufficient, but it does mean being able to find appropriate help when needed.

That evening I slept in a small trading post in Pang that consisted of a few tents with food and a floor for the night. Again there were no other foreigners.

Around sunset, while strolling around the camp, I looked at the sky, the stream and the mountains with a fresher eye – no doubt born of the realisation that I'd soon be leaving India. It'd be very difficult to find an ugly place in the Himalayas, but neither was this small trading post the most beautiful. Nevertheless it moved me to a greater extent than some of the more spectacular scenery I'd seen.

I was in a valley at an altitude of 4,600 metres, surrounded by mountains made of ochre-coloured scree that rose another 1,000 metres. There was no permanent habitation within 100km and the stony ground only supported the odd spiny bush that grew no more than a few inches high. The incessant wind carried the sounds of the bells of the few pack ponies that could survive here. The wind also carried sand, creating convoluted and surreal sculptures that rose up from the valley of rubble like arthritic fingers rising from a palm. What a beautiful world we live in. And how lucky I am to have seen a bit of it.

~~~~~~~~~~

The next morning I didn't feel quite so full of wonder.

The previous night, some soldiers from the nearby camp had come to my tent for an evening of distilled barley juice and merrymaking. They'd invited me to join them, but I felt it wiser to decline. In hindsight, if I'd joined them perhaps I wouldn't have minded so much that they didn't leave until one o'clock in the morning.

When they finally left, I dozed off – only to be awakened when a big truck pulled into camp. It reversed up to my tent with its exhaust pipe only inches from my face. To cap it all, at six o'clock in the morning the driver warmed up the engine for half an hour before setting off.

So the next day, all bleary-eyed and stinking of diesel, I decided it wasn't such a wonderful world after all.

A strong cup of tea and an omelette for breakfast revived me somewhat, and I set off for the next leg. By three o'clock in the afternoon I reached a broken bridge over a river. I'd been told about this obstacle by the leader of the American and British biker group, but he'd assured me the river could be forded.

The river was sizeable – about 30 metres wide – and tumbling down the mountainside; it looked quite deep and fast to me. I decided to wait for another vehicle to come up the road in case I needed some help. A few minutes later, a truck arrived and I stopped it. I asked the driver if he could wait on the other side until I'd crossed.

With a big smile, he nodded. 'Yes, no problem.'

I watched him cross the water, wave out of the window... and drive on.

Although prudence told me I should wait for another vehicle, after 10 minutes I decided I could manage it alone. After all, I was a proper biker now; I'd been on the road for months and I'd managed crossings through snowfields and landslides. I braced myself, kick-started the bike, gathered some speed, and rode into the river. Two-thirds of the way across, in the deepest part of the river, I stalled.

Big Thumper's front wheel was lodged between two rocks. I tried pushing the bike forward, I tried rocking it backwards, I tried leaning over in the water to dislodge the rocks with my hands... but nothing worked. Eventually I resigned myself to standing knee-deep in freezing-cold water, and I did so with my finger on the horn whilst concentrating on keeping the bike upright in the fast-moving current.

Fortunately, a few minutes later, a truck pulled up and the passenger waded through the water to help me. Not even the two of us together could push it out, so the driver came to help too. I was so grateful.

Wet, cold and shaken, I sat on the roadside, wrung my socks out and caught my breath. Eventually, I prepared to push the bike up to a rest tent only one kilometre further on, where I could stay for the night and let it dry out.

Just for the hell of it I tried kick-starting the bike and, amazingly, on the second try, it fired up. Over ten minutes in the water, with the exhaust pipe completely submerged and the battery half-submerged, and still it started. Now *that's* impressive. I bet the fancy Japanese bikes couldn't do that...

In the morning, as I was fitting my luggage into the racks, a luxury Mercedes tour bus from England pulled up. We'd been passing each other on the road for the last two days. I told them about my river adventure and showed them the state of my engine oil – actually more water than oil. The tour leader, Simon, shook his head and offered to change it for me. My first reaction was not to chance it: what if he opened the engine up and for some reason couldn't get it back together? I was only four hours away from the nearest mechanic. But then I accepted Simon knew what he was talking about, since he was both the driver and mechanic for the tour. He seemed a better bet than chancing it on a difficult road with an engine full of water.

While his tour group waited, he changed the oil, and the rest of my day's journey was pleasantly uneventful. Quite a change from recent days of wobbly wheels, broken clutch levers and river crossings! I hoped this was the beginning of a new trend – even though I didn't really expect it to be.

Chapter 20
Packing up in Delhi

The improvised spacer made out of the inner ring of a ball bearing didn't, in fact, get me back to Delhi. But it did get me out of Ladakh and to the town of Rampur, where I knew I could find help from the local mechanic. I'd already met him last November when my decompressor cable had come out of its socket.

By the time I pulled up to his garage, the wobble in my back wheel was very noticeable. The mechanic was very amused when I showed him the improvised spacer. True, it had got me from Leh to Rampur, but it had also ruined the cushion rubbers and the two ball bearings in the back wheel.

He also laughed when he discovered that my chain, sprockets and ball bearings were Enfield copies. I wouldn't mind so much, except that they were replaced in the official Enfield dealership in Lucknow; one of those that has signs on the walls warning against cheap Enfield imitations.

Unfortunately, with so much movement in the back wheel, I'd found it very tiring controlling the bike and had not enjoyed the ride down to Rampur. It had taken all my concentration to keep the bike upright, and the few times I did let my mind wander, I started imagining all sorts of accidents.

I did have some pleasant moments too, though. One night I'd stopped in a small mountain town with a guesthouse over the bus station. Like in most countries, bus stations in India seem to attract the seedier elements; the damp, smelly room allocated to me gave onto a balcony occupied by a group of men drinking alcohol. The expression on my face must have made clear my reservations: the guesthouse owner suggested I may prefer to take a spare bedroom in his family home instead.

Gratefully I accepted and he invited me in. The house was built around a courtyard with a Hindu shrine in the middle. His parents were away at a wedding, but his two sisters, aged 15 and 17, spent the afternoon with me. They taught me how to make chapatis and giggled at my mis-shaped attempts, looked through my toiletry bag, showed me their make-up and applied pearly pink varnish to my nails.

After Rampur, I continued towards Delhi. I was now only 250km from the capital on India's main highway (the four-laned Grand Trunk Road) and the temptation to open the throttle was very strong. Only the persistent monsoon rain and the knowledge that most accidents occur near the final destination restrained me from going for the maximum 120km per hour, when I knew the speedometer needle, and the rest of the bike, would start shaking violently.

Suddenly I heard a rattle and lost all acceleration, as well as all my gears. The chain had broken. Was my journey going to end in the ignominy of having to load the bike into a truck? No: I'd find a way to deal with this myself. I unloaded the bike and took out my tool box and a spare chain link.

As I bent over to start the job, two men on a Honda Hero (a 100cc motorcycle) stopped to help. They suggested that rather than try to do it myself, I should go to a mechanic just three kilometres away. They even offered to push my bike there. But I refused; for once I wanted to solve my own mechanical problem. And anyway, I couldn't ask two strangers to push 200kg of bike all the way there. They were insistent, though, and explained that they'd use their own bike to push me. So off we went, the two men riding behind me and slightly to the side whilst the rider placed his leg on my bike's frame.

In just a few minutes we reached the mechanic, who quickly repaired the chain. The two men then invited me to come to their house for lunch. My first reaction was to decline; many times I'd been invited by men like this, and every time I'd refused because I was afraid they might see my acceptance as a come-on. But now my trip was almost finished and I'd never have another invitation like this. I checked their wives would be at home and accepted. In the end, I stayed overnight in their home.

One of the men, Balwan, was visiting his family for the summer. He'd emigrated to Italy two years previously, where he worked in a foundry. Although my Italian is bad, it's much better then my Hindi, so we managed to have reasonably coherent conversations.

I'm not quite sure how Balwan had managed to obtain a work permit for Italy, but he nonetheless had one, which he proudly showed me. I understood it had involved using, and paying, an agent who'd arranged all the paperwork. Balwan hoped his wife and two children would be able to join him the following year.

He also bragged that he made over $1,000 a month – a huge salary by Indian standards – although I thought it must still have been difficult to support himself as well as send money home. Despite this, he only had good things to say about Italy; so much so I should think his friends and relatives in India must have been getting sick of hearing how much better things were there. He compared the telephone systems, the electricity grids, the state of the roads, the quality of the coffee and so on.

I thought he'd gone too far when he reprimanded his cousin for burping after a meal: a perfectly acceptable custom in India. Shamed, his cousin apologised to me, thus also embarrassing me.

The next day, the families tried to make me stay. It took me over an hour to convince them that I really did want to leave. Eventually, the two men escorted me to the main road and bought me a juice before I set off. We sat under a corrugated iron roof while Balwan talked with friends. While they spoke together in Hindi, I watched the traffic negotiate the monsoon rain. There was a lot of joking and laughing among the men – none of which I could understand.

I asked Balwan to translate into Italian.

'One of my friends says he recently met a Western woman and she had very large breasts. He wants to know why you don't.'

Good question.

~~~~~~~~~~

I rode up to Delhi in heavy rain and arrived at my final destination soaked right through. Delhi was still as confusing to me as it had been the first time, with its hundreds of roundabouts. It was rush-hour and I had no idea how to get to the YMCA.

At a red light I stopped alongside a white Maruti car to ask directions to 'CP'. I was trying to impress the driver with my local knowledge: only locals call Connaught Place 'CP'. As I'd hoped, he said, 'Follow me.'

He was a young man keen to show off his driving, and it took all my skills to keep up with his weaving in and out. At the next light, he rolled down his window and asked, over the noise of the traffic, 'Where are you going?'

'The YMCA. It's just off CP,' I shouted back.

'Are you staying there?'

'Yes.'

He pointed to the young woman sitting in the passenger seat. 'My girlfriend is asking if you want to go see a movie with us?'

I thought, Why not?

We went to my hotel, where my two new friends waited for me to check in and change into dry clothes.

Ritu was a petite woman of 24 who worked as a quality controller for an Indian company that exported clothes to the US. I was amused – but not surprised – to hear that their American client had asked that the Indian manufacturer leave out the zip fasteners from the finished product: every single item I'd bought in India (jacket, trousers, bag) had the zip break in a matter of days. As

Ritu's boyfriend, Jai, put it: 'India can make the atomic bomb but not zips.'

We rode in Jai's car to the cinema theatre, but it was sold out so instead they took me to the five-star Ashok Hotel for a drink, and we toasted the end of my trip with a spicy Bloody Mary.

Ritu and Jai spoke about their relationship.

'We've known each other for two years,' Ritu told me.

Since tact has never been one of my strong points, I asked, 'Do your parents know about your relationship?'

'No,' Ritu replied.

'Do they know that Jai exists?'

'No, he never calls me at home. I call him on his mobile and sometimes he'll call me at work. But I don't like that because people there will start talking.'

'What would your parents say if they knew?'

Ritu answered, 'Mine would be very angry to learn I had a boyfriend, but I think they would like him. With Jai's parents it would be more difficult.'

She glanced over to Jai, who looked down at his drink. 'They are very important people and my family is not so rich. I think they will want to arrange a suitable wife for him.'

~~~~~~~~~~~

Over the next few days I met other young Delhiites via an Enfield motorcycle club, and was re-introduced to such delights of modern civilisation as ice-cream, pizzas, lamb hamburgers and the excessive consumption of alcohol.

Following a particularly heavy night, I took an early train for a day trip to Agra to visit the Taj Mahal. Unfortunately my eyes found the light bouncing off the white marble too bright, and my ears found the 'ohhs' and 'ahhs' of admiring visitors too loud to appreciate the magic of the building.

And anyway, I was preoccupied with Big Thumper. I'd planned on giving it a complete overhaul, repainting it, re-chroming it and shipping it home. In the end, however, I decided to sell it.

It was reading Robert Pirsig's *Zen and the Art of Motorcycle Maintenance* that did it. In it, the author explains that there are two types of people: the romantics (the *Zen* part of the title) and the classics (the *motorcycle maintenance* part of the title). Romantics are interested in the pleasure of riding a bike, while classics are interested in the pleasure of understanding how the bike works.

If there's one thing my trip taught me it's that, according to Pirsig's definition, I'm a romantic – which is definitely the wrong character type for a bike such as the Enfield. This bike requires a lot of maintenance: the points, the tappets, the carburettor, the chain, the nuts and bolts; they all need regular checking. And although this hadn't been too much of a problem in India, where I was never far from a mechanic, at home it would mean having to learn how to do it all myself. And if I hadn't learned it on this trip, when would I ever learn?

Anyway, I decided the thrill would be greater, and the sense of adventure stronger, if the motorbike retained its mystery. Knowing about combustion and compression, valves and tappets would demystify the riding experience and reduce my Enfield to a mechanical machine.

Not a responsible attitude, I know, but it worked for me.

With the monsoon rain washing away a tear, I said goodbye to Big Thumper at Nana Motors – an Enfield dealer beneath the Hilton flyover in Delhi.

Epilogue
December 2014

From a distance of almost two decades, I look at the thirty-something woman in this book with a great deal of amusement – and also a lot of exasperation. I'm amazed by how lucky she was to do this journey and to finish it in one piece. Although I'm still a romantic at heart, I now know that a little motorbike maintenance goes a long way.

My year-long journey was the most intense period of my life: every day seemed longer, brighter, richer. I suppose it was a belated coming-of-age, where I learned that every journey, by definition, is into the unknown; an unknown full of choices, opportunities and – perhaps most importantly – near misses.

As a result of this journey, I fell in love with John. We sometimes joke that if I'd had a selfie stick I wouldn't have stopped and asked him to take my picture. (A perfect example of the isolating impact of technology...)

I didn't know it at the time, but India turned out to be a fortuitous choice of destination. Winston Churchill once said about Russia that it was a 'riddle wrapped in a mystery inside an enigma'. To me, that also accurately describes India. Perhaps if I'd travelled more slowly, learnt Hindi, been more spiritually inclined, or just more aware and reflective, I wouldn't be saying that. But I remain baffled by India: it's the most foreign – and wondrous – place I've ever known. And for that I'm deeply grateful; the world is indeed an amazing place.

Every now and then I wonder what Big Thumper's up to. I'd like to think it's somewhere in the Himalayas, going up a dirt track...

~~~~~~~~~~~~~

About the author

Michèle Harrison was born in France in 1964 to American parents and at the age of 13 moved to London, where she has stayed, more or less, ever since. Travel has always been a big part of her life: she has spent a few years in northern California, a year in Egypt, a year in India and the odd weeks, or months, here and there. She now shares her time between the French Alps and London.

And a final word from the author...

As an independent writer (a more polite way of saying self-published writer) it can be difficult to get talked about. Therefore, if you can find the time to leave a review on the site where you bought this book, I'd be very grateful.

I really enjoy hearing from readers so please feel free to contact me directly at indiamotorcycle@gmail.com